Buried Spirituality

A report on the findings of
The Fellowship in the Spirituality of Young People
based at Sarum College, Salisbury

Phil Rankin

Published by Sarum College Press.

ISBN 0 9534836 9 X

Sarum College Press
19 The Close, Salisbury
Wiltshire SP1 2EE
01722 326899
bookshop@sarum.ac.uk
www.sarumcollegebookshop.co.uk

Cover photograph taken from original graffiti. Artist unknown.

Contents

FOREWORD

I have been working with young people in many different guises for some fifteen years - in conflict resolution, community building, detached work, schools work, centre-based work, social education, drugs, alcohol and sex education, sports coaching. I also happen to have a continuously developing set of beliefs, and for quite a number of years I have been thinking about the implications of my work for these beliefs, and in turn of my beliefs for any work. On every occasion that I have encountered young people it has been clear that they have values and beliefs and a way of existing in the world that I want others to be able to experience and be affected by.

This Fellowship has afforded me that opportunity. I have been able to engage with young people and hear their stories, their feelings, their values, their beliefs, their understandings. I only hope that I have fully done justice to the invaluable time that young people allowed me to spend with them. Above all else I hope that in this report you will be able to hear young people and that in hearing, you will fully listen and be affected by what young people have said these past three years.

Before I turn to the body of the report, I wish to record my thanks to the Sir Halley Stewart Trust for their generous support of this fellowship. In particular I want to thank Leslie Griffiths for his insights, encouragement and the time that he afforded to me during the time of this Fellowship. It was with considerable wisdom and foresight that Sarum College was chosen as the most suitable place to situate the Fellowship. The freedom, trust and support of Sarum College has been especially valuable to the Fellowship and moreover, to me personally. The Fellowship has also benefited greatly from its advisers who, while they did not always share my personal perspectives, willingly offered their time and expertise: John Baxter-Brown, David Durston, Diana

4

Greenfield, Tim Macquiban, Richard Proctor, Philip Richter, Paul Rolph, Ellie Tompkins, Peter Tyler.

Finally of course, I owe the utmost thanks to those young people who were willing to participate and to spend so much of their time in conversation with me. It was an absolute privilege to be able to hear their voices. It is they who form the main story of this report.

Phil Rankin   June 2005
Sarum College,
19, The Close,
Salisbury,
England

prankin@sarum.ac.uk

Background

The often-gloomy scene regarding young people and Christianity is well documented. Christian religious affiliation in England, Scotland and Wales has decreased quite dramatically,[1] Northern Ireland shows clear signs of following a similar path[2] and other faiths do not escape this apparent decline. Although less than 2% of the whole population claim a non-Christian identity, the evidence suggests that commitment to the institutions of these faiths is also weakening.[3] These developments are especially interesting when it is realised that the number of employed church based youth workers is at an all time high and that the provision through parachurch agencies is also increasing.[4]

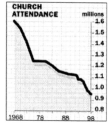

Figure One: Church Attendance in England[5]

There is of course research suggesting that there are many people who do not use traditional institutions as an expression of their faith.[6] While this may be true Bruce argues, "...that three things are causally related: the social importance of religion, the number of people who take it seriously, and how seriously anyone takes it....the declining social significance of religion causes a decline in the number of religious people and the extent to which people are religious."[7] If you consider the table above alongside Bruce's suggestion that as less people take religion seriously its social significance declines, in turn resulting in even less people taking religion seriously, things do not really look like becoming any more positive for religion in the future.

Alongside these changes in religious affiliation and attendance, "Survey after survey shows that increasing numbers of people now prefer to call themselves 'spiritual' rather than 'religious'."[8] This has been reflected by changes in education and work with young people. The 1988 Education Reform Act required schools to promote the spiritual development of pupils at school and of society.[9] Although there have been developments since, most notably in 1993, it is of note that in 1977 the Supplement to Curriculum 11-16 provided two definitions of spirituality whereas each of the other areas of development is given only one. Youth work has faced similar dilemmas, and in recent years alterations in aims and objectives relating to spirituality have taken place. Debate about the place of spirituality, and of religion, in education and in youth work is still continuing.

It is this context that created the desire to reflect upon the spirituality of young people in the U.K. A proposal was prepared at the invitation and with the support of the Sir Halley Stewart Trust.[10] Aims and objectives were developed that enabled and encouraged the use of innovative data collection methods and the Sir Halley Stewart Trust supported these by providing the project the time, finances and freedom to undertake such a task.

The Fellowship in the Spirituality of Young People was created and then situated at Sarum College, Salisbury.[11] The College aims to be a place of 'living theology' and has a growing reputation as a provider of both academic and experiential courses. It also has strong relationships with numerous institutions and individuals and as an ecumenical institution it has been ideally placed to house this project.

It was hoped that by gaining a better understanding of the spirituality of young people, individuals and agencies, both religious and secular, might be better equipped to target resources in the vital task of relating to young people. The principal aims of the Fellowship were:

- To explore with young people their experiences and perspectives of spirituality. This would include young people's perceptions of themselves and others as well as their understandings and use of terms such as spirituality, spiritual, and religion.

- To explore with young people the meanings and interpretations that they identify for themselves from various media, and the impact such interpretations have upon their personal and corporate sense of identity.

- To explore how young people develop their sense of values in a multi-cultural society, and discover with young people the responses, if any, offered by Christian faith.

Although there is even more that could be written than will be contained here, the following chapters will consider in detail the methodology used, the responses made by young people and some of the implications of these. I think that you will find the methodology to be innovative and the findings striking. In the next chapter some definitions of spirituality will be outlined and, although this is perhaps the most complex chapter of this text, it does set the remainder in context.

[1]"Whereas 12% of the English population went to church weekly each Sunday in 1979, and 10% in 1989, this has dropped to 7.5% in 1998." (Brierly, P (2000) *The Tide Is Running Out* Christian Research, Page 9)

"The number of worshippers in the Church of Scotland declined by 17000 in 2004, according to the latest figures." (The Times, May 7th, 2005, *Faith News*)

"The proportion of the total Welsh population attending church declined from 14.6 per cent in 1982 to 8.7 per cent in 1995." (The Bible Society)

[2] Northern Ireland shows significantly different figures to the other parts of the U.K. but there is still clear evidence of decline. Figures in the 2001 census are in some cases very different from (usually higher than) the Churches' own figures. This may well be due to the readiness of some census respondents in Northern Ireland to identify themselves with religious denominations with which they are not actively involved or to use religious terms to describe their cultural, national and political allegiance. From the 2001 Census, 85.9% of the population of Northern Ireland identify with some denomination of the Christian Church. However, this figure is more comparable with the 71.9% of the people in England and Wales who identified themselves as Christian. It is suggested that actual participation in church has dropped from 44% in 1989 to 30% in 2002. (Social Attitudes Survey, University Of Ulster, 2004)

[3] See Bruce, S. (1995) *Religion in Modern Britain* Oxford University Press. Also Davie, G. (1994) *Religion in Britain Since 1945: Believing Without Belonging* Blackwell

[4] Baxter-Brown, J. (2003) *The Matrix Conference A Report on a Questionnaire Survey* C.T.E.

[5] The Times March 5th, 2005, *Liberal and Weak Clergy Blamed for Empty Pews*

[6] See Davie, G. (1994) *Religion in Britain Since 1945: Believing Without Belonging* Blackwell. Also, Richter, P. & Francis, L. J. (1998) *Gone But Not Forgotten: Church Leaving And Returning* Dartman, Longman & Todd

[7] Bruce, S. (2002) *God is Dead, Secularization in the West* Blackwell Publishing, Page 3

[8] Heelas, Paul & Woodhead, Linda (2005) *The Spiritual Revolution* Blackwell, Page 1

[9] This was along with moral, physical, mental and cultural development.

[10] www.sirhalleystewart.org

[11] www.sarum.ac.uk

Understanding Terms

Spirituality. This may be a word that we all recognise but, as Jones, Wainwright and Yarnold say, "Spirituality...is a vague word, often used with no clear meaning, or with a wide and vague significance."[12] While many have tried to define spirituality, it remains something of a nebulous subject. We talk of people who show spirit, as if it is a personality trait. We talk of sports people putting in a spirited display during competition. We talk of things being spirited away when they move unexpectedly or quickly. We talk of speaking in a spirit of truth. But these uses are not necessarily connected to 'spiritual' or 'spirituality.'

It is interesting to note the change in the use of the terms 'spirituality' and 'spiritual', coming a lot more into the mainstream in recent years. There are now numerous journals with *spirituality* in the title, while some 30 years ago there were very few. There was even a recent television advert for shampoo that pointed out the shampoo wouldn't give the user 'some deep cleansing spiritual experience'!

It would be relatively straightforward to understand spirituality in specifically Christian terms but this would not come close to presenting a true picture of the spirituality of young people across the United Kingdom. David Hay writes in *Spirit of the Child*, "...Western researchers who have looked at spirituality have almost always focused on the language of Christianity as the criterion for identifying their subject... this kind of limitation is in danger of distorting the accuracy of the findings very seriously." [13]

The decline in participation in the long-established religions in the West has coincided with research by the Religious Experience Research Centre, among others, that would suggest that there is something inherent in every human person. Alister Hardy, after retiring from a Chair of Zoology at Oxford, set up the Religious Experience Research Centre and proposed a disciplined study of firsthand religious or transcendent experiences among human beings because there was, and generally still is, a widespread belief that such experiences are rare and that people who report to have such experiences are poorly educated, are from socially deprived backgrounds and are unhappy.

Hardy argued that human development was not an entirely mechanical process and that it was initially directed by deliberate alterations in habit, which he termed 'internal' or 'behavioural' selection. He believed that the forerunners of the human species discovered a relationship to a transcendent presence that had the potential to pervade all experience, and that this is a biological predisposition which is universal. In Hardy's opinion the biological reason for the selection of this predisposition was because it had survival value for the individual.

In agreement with Hardy's proposal, Rappaport writes, "It is both plausible and prudent to assume, at least initially, that anything which is universal to human culture is likely to contribute to human survival. Phenomena that are merely incidental, or peripheral, or epiphenomenal to the mechanisms of survival are hardly likely to become universal, nor to remain so, if they do."[14]

When commenting on the work of Alister Hardy, David Hay writes, "...the universality of report of religious experience is inclined from time to time to make the biologist sit up and take notice...if accounts of such experience are so widespread and become part of the central meaning systems of practically every culture, it takes more than a sophisticated sneer to dismiss it all as illusion."[15] While it would be incorrect to assume that spirituality is simply religious or transcendent experience, it is none the less clear that there is something universal to humanity. What is not so clear is how this *something* might be understood.

It is suggested that spirituality should be understood as the realm of the non-material, such as a belief in the transcendent or in God, something perhaps otherworldly.[16] By this understanding of spirituality, the individual who understands the world in physical terms, or at least dismisses the idea of some kind of spiritual realm or the existence of a transcendent being, cannot have spirituality. If it is correct that there is *something* inherent in all humans, then any definition must be open enough to include everyone, not just those who understand the world in predominantly religious terms. Any understanding of spirituality must move beyond the boundaries of Christianity, and any faith system for that matter, but it also must not become so narrow as to exclude religious ways of life.

David Elkins advocates that spirituality is something multi-dimensional and attempts to distinguish it from religiosity. In the various dimensions of spirituality, he contends that a spiritual person has 'an experientially based belief' that there is a transcendent dimension to life and defines spirituality in this way:

"Spirituality, which comes from the Latin *spiritus*, meaning "breath of life", is a way of being and experiencing that comes about through awareness of a transcendent dimension and that is characterised by certain identifiable values in regard to self, others, nature, life and whatever one considers to be the Ultimate"[17]

He suggests that there are some forces in contemporary Western culture which inhibit spiritual growth, as well as pointing to some ways that people have felt that growth has taken place. Each identified path to spirituality has its own positive and negative aspects. For example, while intimate relationships may be paths to the sacred, they may also be used for control of one person by another, and can be destructive rather than constructive. Elkins goes on to list a number of attributes of spirituality, many of which are very prescriptive. He suggests that spirituality must contain an awareness of sacred in life, a sense of awe and wonder, even that a person must be a visionary.

It seems to me that Elkins largely defines spirituality in terms of values and that these are values that he has decided 'help' people to be better people e.g. more purposeful, impact on others, visionary, does not seek ultimate satisfaction from money and possessions etc. Elkins' definition has been developed within the fields of psychology and theology, and it is the theological or religious emphasis that makes it unsatisfactory. The difficulty is the prominence given to an awareness of a transcendent dimension. As I expressed earlier, while there is research to show that there is *something* universal in humanity, if this *something* is defined with the emphasis on a transcendent dimension then anyone who does not recognise a transcendent dimension cannot be considered to have spirituality.

Similar to Elkins, Fisher suggests that the increasing interest in spirituality in the West has a lot to do with the desire for a whole and integrated life, with people searching for a sense of unity and purpose in life. Fisher defines spirituality in terms of something that 'helps' people, particularly with their health. He distinguishes between spirituality and religion saying that religion focuses on ideology and rules of faith and belief systems while spirituality focuses on experience and relationships. Spirituality is usually seen as having to do with the individual, while religion is oriented around institutions and organisations. Fisher also points out that research has drawn attention to the importance of spirituality in human health and well being.[18]

At its core Fisher defines spirituality as, "...a fundamental dimension of peoples' overall health and well-being"[19] and identifies four domains of spirituality: personal, communal, environmental and global. He suggests that these are all focused on relationships and improvement in health and well being, and argues that developing positive relationships in each domain enhances spiritual health. However, because of the importance of the inter-relationship between the various domains, overall health has to do with the combined effect of spiritual well being in *each* domain.

Like the previous understandings this one is quite limiting. The focus on spirituality as a dimension of health and the complete rejection of religion being an aspect of spirituality, create a situation that is much too restrictive. Improved health is perhaps a by-product of spirituality, but it is not spirituality in its entirety. In the same way that vitamin C provides health benefits, so might spirituality. But both vitamin C and spirituality exist in their own right and are not just dimensions or aspects of health.

To distinguish between religion and spirituality in the way that Fisher does creates what appears to be a superiority of one over the other. Indeed an individual's religion organised around systems and institutions may actually be an expression of spirituality. Spirituality is not necessarily some feelings orientated aspect of life that is set in contrast to religion. An institutionalised religion is as likely to be an expression of spirituality as is a 'touchy-feely, pick-and-mix' spirituality.

Although there are countless numbers of other understandings of spirituality, the only other that I wish to discuss here is that of Sandra M. Schneiders. She understands, "...spirituality as the experience of conscious involvement in the project of life integration through self transcendence toward the ultimate value one perceives."[20] Schneiders herself suggests that this understanding is broad enough to include both religious and nonreligious spiritualities but also, "specific enough to exclude aimless spontaneity, partial projects or religious dilettantism."[21] The essential elements of spirituality as Schneiders defines it are conscious effort, the goal of life integration, self-transcendence and the finalisation of the project by ultimate value.

In consideration of this understanding it must first be recognized that the term experience is itself something that is difficult to define. In this circumstance it firstly suggests that spirituality is a personal lived reality, something of which one is aware. It is not just a collection of repetitive practices, but is a way of life that is pursued, ongoing and is reflected upon. One doesn't necessarily have to name that experience spirituality, but one must be aware of and consciously involved in the experience.

Schneiders suggests that spirituality is not solely an episodic event such as being overwhelmed by a beautiful sunset or practices such as saying prayers, rubbing crystals, or going to church. The consciousness of an experience might indeed include going to church or being overwhelmed by a beautiful sunset but the significant thing is that any experience must be part of an ongoing process and not just a one-off event with no reflection or integration into life.

That is to say that an action is just an action, an experience just an experience, only becoming part of spirituality when reflected upon. Spirituality is focused toward ultimate value and any experience is understood in relation to that spirituality. The action or experience has a particular meaning because of the spirituality that one might bring to that experience, and one's future spirituality is affected by the action or experience. It is entirely circular. What is suggested by this definition, differently to the others that have been reflected upon, is that there is a clear distinction between spiritual experiences, indeed any experience, and spirituality. Without getting into a full discussion about the definition of a spiritual experience, I want to offer the following by way of example:

Two people are standing on a mountainside on a beautiful evening as the sun is setting. One person describes the experience and says that he/she felt in touch with themselves, with the world around them and with God and describes the experience as spiritual. The second person describes the experience and says that he/she was standing on a mountainside on a beautiful evening as the sun was setting.

While this is an entirely fictitious example, it simply shows that two people involved in the same event do not necessarily have the same experience and that this experience is affected by something else, something *outside* the event itself. In my view that *something else* is spirituality. If you will, spirituality could be likened to glasses through which one sees (experiences) the world and experiences in the world in turn affect the glasses through which ones sees (experiences) the world. Any experience, whether it could be described as spiritual or not, is not spirituality until the experience is reflected upon. Every experience, no matter how it might be described, remains an experience and entirely separate from spirituality until it is integrated into life. In a sense, what difference does it make to the individual concerned? What significance does it have?

I think that some of the apparent confusion in defining spirituality arises because of this particular issue. There is a clear distinction between spirituality, spiritual and spiritual experience and with this distinction comes a much clearer understanding of all three terms. Spirituality is something that is universal to all humanity, it is something that is inherent. Even the very denial of a spiritual realm, a transcendent being, God etc. is in my opinion evidence of spirituality, but this is not evidence of transcendent, spiritual or religious experience.

In consideration of the term 'spiritual', I think that this whole area would be much more concise if it were understood that to be spiritual is little different from say, being sporty or being a snowboarder. It is something that people do (e.g. they may engage in *spiritual* activities such as praying) and is to a great extent synonymous with religion (e.g. people are said to be *spiritual* because they pray). Being known as spiritual or defining yourself in this way is simply an indicator of spirituality in the same way as being known as a Goth might be an indicator of spirituality. To be spiritual is perhaps another indicator of spirituality, but spiritual and spirituality are not the same thing and should not be confused.

The emphasis on reflection evident in Schneiders' definition could lead to the suggestion that she understands spirituality as an entirely cognitive activity. However, this issue only arises because of incorrect interpretations of knowledge and of the person. Interpreting reflection as an entirely cognitive activity occurs only if the person is divided into separate aspects such as mind and body and it is believed that the only way of knowing is in the mind. Although there is not opportunity to expand upon this issue here, suffice to say that people have knowledge more broadly than just in the mind (e.g. love is *felt knowledge* as much as cognitive knowledge) and are much more integrated and interdependent than any separation of the person allows.

Upon initial reading it appears that this emphasis on reflection means that spirituality is entirely subjective, and in today's society individual recognition and definition appears centrally important. "It is now generally accepted that we live in an age which no longer respects any sense of ultimate or absolute authority. The title of the Manic Street Preachers' album, *This is my truth tell me yours*, has become something of a cliché in describing the relativism of postmodernity. The all-encompassing, over-arching narrative which gave meaning to the whole of life has been replaced with the local or personal narrative which gives meaning to my existence or that of my community."[22]

While the idea that there existed a time where an *'all-encompassing, over-arching narrative'* is certainly disputable, the reality of contemporary society is that the individual is supreme.

Self-definition and meaning appears to be most important. However, when it comes to defining and understanding spirituality it cannot be left entirely to each individual person to decide what is spirituality, and what is not. This would create a situation where anything and everything could be considered spirituality, thus making it practically meaningless. At the same time, any understanding cannot be too restrictive, as this will not allow for the full range and diversity of understandings and experiences.

While maintaining a subjective, individual feature, Schneiders' definition also contains an element of objective criteria in defining spirituality. For instance, if a person suggests that stroking their puppy is spirituality then this is subjective. However, the objective criteria of conscious involvement, and life integration through self-transcendence, must then be applied. The project of life integration suggests that spirituality is holistic, involving all of an individuals being. It is an attempt to bring all life together in an integrated blend of ongoing growth and development. It involves one's life as a whole in relation to reality in its totality: body and spirit, emotions and thought, social and individual aspects of life.

A significant aspect of this life integration is the reflection upon any experience and the effort to incorporate that reflection into one's worldview. The experience may derive from an element of practice such as going to church, praying etc., which is both informed and subsequently informing of spirituality. The way of life and ultimate value is then affected by the experience and any new experience is once again reflected upon and integrated into life. In this way it is a continuous and consistent aspect of development.

At its simplest, self-transcendence is an 'effort' to become. In a sense, what you are not, you are becoming. For example, if I perceive myself to not be a nice person, but I want to be a nice person then I will go beyond myself (self-transcend) to learn to become nice. As Schneiders says, "It is the capacity of persons...through knowledge and love...to reach beyond themselves in relationship to others and thus become more than self-enclosed material monads."[23] In her view, self-transcendence is not just about the 'I' but also about the 'we'; it is about how we go the extra step for others as well as ourselves.

In his hierarchy of human needs Maslow places self-actualisation at the top, suggesting that this is becoming everything that you are capable of becoming. On the basis of his research he described self-actualisers as, "Perceptive, emotionally open, natural and spontaneous, problem-centred, rather than self-centred, happy with their own company, autonomous, self-accepting and other-accepting rather than over-critical and judgmental, appreciative of life, capable of deep and loving relationships, humorous, creative, ethical, democratic and consistent."[24] Self-transcendence is the full realisation of oneself and ones potential and, as is clear from Maslow's list, is as much about relationship to others and the world around us as it is about our awareness of self.

In consideration of the ultimate value it might be suggested that each of us has a system of numerous values rather than a single ultimate value. However, Schneiders might actually be correct here. Although we do all appear to live according to a series of values, or even ultimate values, I suspect that these can still be subsumed within one 'macro-value'. For example, the Ten Commandments might be considered as a series of values but it seems some are more primary than others, that some are logical consequences of others. For instance, to not steal or not commit adultery could be said to ultimately derive from the first commandments about God. If one starts to strip away some of the apparent value system, eventually an Ultimate Value from which others derive may be found. In a way, it is like always asking 'why?' - 'Why not steal?'...'Because stealing hurts other people' would suggest that the value is actually other people's welfare. 'But why do other people matter?'...'Because God made them', or 'Because what goes around comes around, and we all have to live together' might be leading towards the Ultimate Value.

In *Dynamics of Faith*, Tillich challenges his readers to consider what has centring power in their lives. The 'god values' in life are the things that concern us ultimately, our ultimate value. As Fowler states, "Our true devotion directs itself toward the objects of ultimate concern. That ultimate concern may centre finally in our own ego or its extensions - work, prestige and recognition, power and influence, wealth. One's ultimate concern may be invested in family, university, nation or church. Love, sex and a loved partner might be the passionate centre of one's ultimate concern."[25] This 'Ultimate Value', 'ultimate concern' or 'god value' shapes how we are and how we invest in our most deep loves.

Although Schneiders uses the word 'toward' in her definition, she is not saying that spirituality necessarily has to be understood as positive. A person's ultimate value may well be based in an anarchist philosophy, a philosophy that others may understand as negative. However, this philosophy is still that person's spirituality. This, in my view, is why perception is vitally important in the area of spirituality. Although from without anarchism may be perceived as a negative spirituality, from within it may be understood positively. The important thing is how the person concerned perceives his or her own ultimate value and spirituality. Whilst others may perceive this chosen way of life differently, it is still spirituality because it derives from that person's perceived ultimate value. A person who might be considered to have anarchist spirituality is still living *towards* their ultimate value - total and absolute freedom without care for order.

I firmly believe that the definition provided by Schneiders - "...the experience of conscious involvement in the project of life integration through self-transcendence toward the ultimate value one perceives." - expresses the full meaning of spirituality and enables clarification of other terms that have been traditionally connected with it. However, one significant problem still remains. Schneiders' definition expresses what is very much a theoretical understanding. In truth this is a criticism that could be levelled at most of the available understandings and definitions.

Ultimately the meaning of any term lies in its use and I do not think that young people will understand or use terms like spiritual, spirituality and spiritual experience within any great degree of theoretical understanding.[26] Perhaps the reality is that in all the efforts to understand and define this spirituality *thing*, it has come to lose any significant or agreed meaning in day-to-day language.

My hope is that in engaging with young people this fellowship will be able to get to grips with how young people use terms like spirituality, spiritual, and spiritual experience, if they use these terms at all. Perhaps there will even be opportunity to simplify these issues and come to a common understanding so that we might all be better equipped to communicate and learn together about spirituality.

[12] Jones, Cheslyn; Wainwright, Geoffrey & Yarnold S.J., Edward. (1986) *The Study of Spirituality* SPCK, Page xxii

[13] Hay, D. with Nye, R. (1998) *The Spirit of the Child* Zondervan, Page 42

[14] Rappaport, R., (1971) *The Sacred in Human Evolution*, Annual Review of Ecology and Systematics, Vol.2, Page 32

[15] Hay, David (1982) *Exploring Inner Space, Is God still possible in the twentieth century?* Penguin Books Ltd., Page 198

[16] See Martin Ashley, Adrian Smith, David Tacey, William O'Malley, Paul Hamill, Michael Yaconelli

[17] Elkins, David N. (1998) *Beyond Religion: 8 Alternative Paths to the Sacred* Quest Books, Page 33

[18] See for example, the work of R. M. Ebst, 1984

[19] Fisher, John (1999) *Making Sense of Spiritual Health and Well-being: Being Human, Becoming Whole,* paper presented at the School of Nursing, University of Ballarat, Page 7

[20] Schneiders, Sandra M. (Fall 1986) T*heology and Spirituality: Strangers, Rivals or Partners?* Horizons 13, Page 266

[21] Schneiders, Sandra M. *Feminist Spirituality: Christian Alternative or Alternative to Christianity?* Page 31

[22] Grayston, John (2002) *The Bible and Spirituality* Scripture Union, Page 100

[23] Schneiders, Sandra M. (Nov. 2003) *Religion vs. Spirituality: A Contemporary Conundrum* Espiritus, Page 165

[24] Maslow, Abraham (1970) *Motivation and Personality* Harper & Row, Page 150

[25] Fowler, James W. (1996) *Faithful Change* Abingdon Press, Page 4

[26] In truth, I am not sure that young people will use these terms in their own conversation at all.

Conversations With Young People

Research took place in the four countries of the United Kingdom (England, Northern Ireland, Scotland and Wales) with an age range of 14 - 25. Aside from the fact that this is the principal age group funded by the Sir Halley Stewart Trust, this age range was chosen because the European Union White Paper of Nov 2001 defines young people within this age bracket and the 2001 United Kingdom Census specifies this age group as a single unit.

A profile matrix was created to ensure a broad representation of participants with reference to age, gender and rural/urban location. The age range was split into four groups,[27] meaning that data would be gathered from 16 groups in each country thus giving a total of 64 groups. The ethnicity, education, employment etc. of every young people was also noted. This secondary information was dependent upon how much detail each participant was willing to give. The researcher regularly assessed the responses of the participants. If particular groups were not represented, or it was thought that certain experiences, perceptions, and understandings that young people hold are not represented, the reasons for this were considered and, if necessary, efforts were made to rectify the situation.

The movements and distribution of young people were mapped in various cities, towns and villages across the U.K with various youth workers, community workers, etc. This was done with reference to rural/urban dynamics in each country and geographical spread (The choice of city, town, or village is partly dependent on the availability of contacts). Colleagues used their knowledge of the area to help map movements of young people, paying particular attention to ensure that information is gathered across various social groups. Effort was made to meet with more than one person in each city, town and village to endeavour to overcome the limitations of one person's knowledge or possible bias.

Although this is time consuming, this type of mapping is necessary so that the young people involved in the research were not only those who were the most obvious and easily accessible. It is relatively straightforward to walk into any town and speak to young people, but using this mapping increased the potential to encounter young people who may not be most easily observed. This enabled the researcher to engage with young people who are not to be found on the main street of many towns and cities in the UK, as well as those who are. The mapping ensured that young people from across the many social groups are represented in the data e.g. Goths, skaters, sports people etc., thus bringing many and varied views to the research. Also, in endeavouring to access a wide range of young people across social groups, one group of young people was often able to explain where another group of young people would be found.

Upon getting some picture of an area, young people were approached in a public space. This took place without the young people being given any prior warning. Young people were approached with the following criteria in mind:

1. It must be a group and not a single individual.

2. It must be in a public space. e.g. park, pub, superstore, café, etc.

3. A group of young people must not be stopped in the street. The group must be stationary and thereby have some ownership over the area that they occupy.

Upon making contact with the group of young people the following steps were followed:

1. The group was asked if they would be willing to participate in some research about young people and their spirituality. If a particular group were unwilling to participate, this would of course be noted.[28]

2. The researcher gave each group of young people information about himself and the subject to be researched. It was emphasised that it is about listening to what they have to say and not to make them into something, evangelise, convert etc. The young people were again asked if they were still willing to participate.

3. The recording process was explained, as was how the information would be used. It was stressed that the process is entirely voluntary and that the conversation can end at any time that the group choose.

4. Everyone was encouraged to participate and to share as freely, openly and honestly as they feel comfortable. It was made clear that this is a conversation and if the young people want to comment on anything that is said or to ask questions of each other, then that would be positive.

5. It was again emphasised that they are free to end the conversation at anytime, for any reason, and that the researcher will leave.

When working with people, regardless of the type of work, awareness of power relationships is essential, as is a high degree of self and spatial awareness. These issues were absolutely central to the development of the chosen methodology. By entering the space of young people, they have the power to refuse to talk or to ask me to leave at anytime. I am obviously entering their space and by so doing, they have ownership of it and confidence in it. Other research has targeted young people in schools but this can create unnecessary power imbalances because the young people have to enter the 'interview room' or similar, rather than someone entering their space.

While there are always internal group relationships to consider, training and experience of facilitation and of young people can help to overcome the internal group pressures. If the correct physical and emotional space and safety is created, people can actually be aided in their willingness to speak for themselves, even if that goes against the thinking of the rest of the group.

To further consider these issues, the interactions with young people should not be understood as interviews. This most certainly could not be the mindset when going to speak with young people. There was no attempt to push young people into an unnatural situation where theories could be tested and investigated. Rather the purpose was to open minds and to create space where dialogue could occur so that we all could learn from and about each other. Equality and awareness of power in the relationships were essential and therefore the interactions are better understood as conversations. I cannot stress enough how important this equality is and how my willingness to learn from young people was absolutely paramount in every single engagement.

With these issues in mind the conversation began with two initial questions:

1. Would you perceive yourself to be spiritual?

2. What do you think the word spiritual means?

The remainder of the conversation was spent exploring and clarifying the young peoples' perceptions of themselves; their understandings of spirituality and how it relates to them; their relationship with and experiences of 'spiritual' activities; their knowledge of the influences upon their perceptions and understandings; and with whom and where they might share their understandings, perceptions and experiences. This part of the conversation was entirely unstructured and therefore yielded different information on each encounter.

When reading research texts and discussing approaches with various individuals I was encouraged to begin the research with *light* questions and this is also the approach encouraged in most youth work training. However, my experience brought me to the opposite conclusion. To return to the short discussion earlier regarding power in relationships, if the correct space and emotional safety exists then most questions will be met with a positive and honest response. For that reason it was decided to begin each conversation with a more personal question about each individual's self-awareness. The introduction was therefore especially important in creating a positive environment enabling each conversation to develop with a high level of openness, confidence and emotional safety.

The recording of each conversation took place immediately the conversation concluded. Considerable time was spent making in-depth notes on what had been discussed. These notes also attempted to detail body language and such things, rather than simply, 'he said, I said'. Awareness of differences between things like thinking/feeling, awareness of God/awareness of an 'other' etc. was also given particular attention. The researcher subsequently typed these notes. All these typed recordings were referenced according to age, gender, and location and all names were changed to preserve anonymity.

This form of recording was chosen for quite a number of reasons but just two will be considered at this point. The first was one of practicality. It was always hoped that this research would be as inclusive as possible. This meant entering environments where using video or tape recording was not feasible. Using such equipment in public spaces does not always provide satisfactory recordings and in bars, restaurants, and cafes the background noise makes this form of recording impossible.

The second issue is related to relationship development. Making notes during the conversations was considered as a recording option but this was rejected as a satisfactory method because of the power issues discussed previously. In working directly with people there are many different types of barriers to overcome e.g. age, gender, ethnicity, education, language etc. especially if the desire is to enable people to talk and share openly and honestly. The use of a notebook can become another unnecessary and very obvious barrier to the creation of a safe, emotional space and create an imbalance of power between the researcher and others to be researched.

Concentrating on taking notes also diminishes the ability to listen. When people are sharing what are often very intimate and private details of their lives that person must be given full attention. To do this the role and emphasis alters during the period of the research. During the conversation rather than being seen at a distance as a 'researcher' or 'interviewer', I become part of that small *society* for a time. Indeed describing the role as that of a facilitator would be a more satisfactory representation of the position within the groups of young people. Upon leaving the group of young people the role changes again to that of researcher. While I am simply outlining role changes, an awareness of these roles is vitally important in giving the voice of each young person due value. Using a notebook in the settings in which the research took place would not come even close to giving full value to the openness that young people presented during each conversation.[29]

Prior to the collect of the main data, the methodology was tested. Conversations took place with approximately 30 young people. These took place in various places, with different social groups in the four countries, and with people of various ages. Detailed recordings of the conversations were made immediately after the conclusion of the interview. A summary of the recordings was passed to approximately 10 other young people and they were asked for their impressions and views of the information. These 'testers' either had similar views or knew of people who had. They expressed surprise at the depth of sharing that had taken place and the honesty with which people appeared to talk.

I also had conversations with three groups of young people in London. A youth worker, with a background in sociology, was also present. He knew the young people and I had met five of them on one previous occasion when we had a very brief conversation after I watched a film that they had made. The meetings were pre-arranged so emphasis was given to the voluntary aspect of the conversation to ensure that the young people were aware that they did not have to participate and could leave at anytime. The remainder of the introduction and conversation took exactly the same form as the process used for the conversations within the body of the research. The colleague who was present wrote a short report on his perspective of the process and the method used.

Some of the comments made were as follows:

"Phil's approach to the work has been careful and considered, with acknowledged personal opinion being placed to one side when discussing the issue of spirituality and the church with young people. Phil is an excellent listener, not giving his own opinions, but listening to what the young people have to say, and then raising appropriate questions to further the discussion."

"I have been impressed by Phil's impartiality and ability to simply ask questions and allow the young people's thoughts to lead the discussion. No opinions were given to lead the young people's responses in any particular direction, nor were the questions structured so as to mislead or re-route their thinking. Phil remained objective throughout. Because of this style the young people were able to explore their own understanding and opinions."

The flexible methodology outlined above opens up my values as the researcher as well as the values of the subjects and allows conversation to take place. I was not there to impose my values and thoughts on others, but merely to bring them into dialogue with young people in order to better know, clarify and understand their values and thoughts. I have always thought this work to be a conversation with others about common interests, with the hope that I may be able to transmit the core of those conversations to a wider public.

Some General Comments

There were a total of 64 groups, 16 groups in each country. In total, there were 211 young people involved: 105 female and 106 male. The conversations took place in a wide variety of settings and with different group sizes. These included:

- Three females in a restaurant in Scotland;

- A brother and sister in an airport in Northern Ireland;

- A male and female in a bookshop in England;

- Two females on a train in Wales.

While there was a full range of education/employment and religious involvement, the sample did not include great variety in ethnicity or disabilities. There were a number of opportunities to engage with young people of different ethnic backgrounds to mine, but these were always as part of a larger group that was predominantly white. This issue had been given consideration when preparing the methodology and the chosen method of data collection, as with any method, has limitations. Although I believe that using this method was and is the most significant way to gather data about spirituality, one of the primary concerns was always safety, both emotional and physical. If young people of various ethnicities had been targeted in their own communities, this could have increased the physical safety risks. This is not to diminish the need for young people from a range of ethnicities to be considered, just that I am perhaps not the most suitable person to undertake such a task. Also, in respect of the emotional safety of the young people, awareness of the difficulties raised by aspects like education, employment, age, gender and ethnicity is vital. In my experience education, employment, age and gender[30] are issues that can be overcome, while ethnicity is sometimes more difficult. In a single random meeting the ethnicity differences could make the spontaneous nature of the research more difficult to maintain.

It has also been suggested by a number of youth workers, both church-based and secular, that different ethnicities may have very different spiritualities. This is something that would require further detailed investigation but was not one of the main aims of this fellowship.

---

[27] The age groups were categorised in this way because of transition periods:
1. 14-16 is GCSE period.
2. 17-18 is A-Level or leaving education/entering employment.
3. 19-21 is University or continuing employment.
4. 22-25 is postgraduate or leaving education/entering education.
[28] This never actually occurred. Not one single group of young people declined to participate
[29] For further discussion of all the issues raised above I would suggest accessing the extensive writings of Carl Rogers. A good place to begin is with the following work: Rogers, C. (1980) *A Way of Being* Houghton Mifflin Company. Another very relevant text is Bellah, R., Madsen, R., Sullivan, W., Swidler, A., Tipton, S. (1996) *Habits of the Heart: Individualism and Commitment in American Life* University of California Press
[30] And religious/political identification in Northern Ireland

Using Grounded Theory

Once all the data was collected, it was analysed using Grounded Theory, a qualitative methodology deriving its name from a practice of generating theory that is 'grounded' in data.

Grounded Theory was formally introduced by the sociologists Barney Glaser and Anselm Strauss in Discovery of Grounded Theory[31] and emerged as an alternative process to more traditional approaches of inquiry that relied heavily on hypothesis testing, verification techniques, and quantitative forms of analysis. Grounded Theory investigates the actualities in the real world and, it is suggested, analyses the data while minimising the impact of any preconceived hypothesis.

Any research could be accused of being idiosyncratic on the basis that any conclusions drawn from the data are from a certain perspective or tradition. Analysts are always, to varying degrees, part of the whole that they are analysing and therefore cannot be value free. No researcher can ever be entirely neutral about the subject that they are analysing. "In framing their problems and interpreting their results, researchers draw on their own experience and their membership in a community of research that is in turn located with specific traditions and institutions."[32] The person undertaking the analysis affects any data analysis and theory development, but using Grounded Theory will diminish the affects of any individual influence.

The purpose of Grounded Theory is not only to describe the voices in the data but also to get to the concepts within the voices by allowing theories to develop. Rather than simply a description of the data, Grounded Theory builds theory using a series of steps. The first step is to conceptualise the data and there can be many dozens of concepts named, possibly even hundreds. Steps two and three develop the concepts into categories and then code these. Reflecting on the relationship between categories, connecting consequences and causal conditions brings categories together. These concepts and categories then lead on to the emergence of theory.

As part of the analysis there was also a process of triangulation whereby 8 people from the Fellowship's Advisory Group used Grounded Theory to analyse half of the data. By considering the data from a number of different perspectives the influence of a single individual can be diminished. It enables findings to be corroborated and although it does not *prove* that any researcher is always right, it does provide further confidence that the findings drawn from the data are not too closely tied to a single perspective.

The members of the Advisory Group involved in the triangulation are involved in a variety of employments, including youth work and education at University level. They were given a half-day input on Grounded Theory to ensure that each individual was analysing by the same process and each member of the Advisory Group then analysed three transcripts prior to a two-day meeting. During the meeting each person analysed a fourth transcript. Thus, in all, 32 transcripts were analysed. Time was then given to the presentation of each individual's findings. Following this a process of coding took place, with each individual inputting into the categorisation.

During the second day I, as the researcher, presented my findings of the same 32 transcripts. I had been present during the process undertaken by the Advisory Group but was there only to record the information and had no input into the process. Following the presentation of my analysis, debate took place to give due consideration to any similarities and differences between my coding and that of the Advisory Group.

The use of Grounded Theory will allow greatest access directly to what young people have had to say and the triangulation provides a strong method of safeguarding against one perspective overly influencing the results. In the following chapters some of the results of the analysis will be detailed and hopefully you will be able to experience something of the valuable time that was spent in the company of young people and hear their voices strongly enough to be impacted and moved by them.

---

[31] Glaser, B. & Strauss, A. (1967) *Discovery of Grounded Theory* Chicago: Aldine
[32] Bellah, R., Madsen, R., Sullivan, W., Swidler, A., Tipton, S. (1996) *Habits of the Heart: Individualism and Commitment in American Life* University of California Press, Page 303

Suzi's Story

In this chapter, before turning to the findings in the totality of the data, we will consider an extended portion of a single conversation transcript. It is quite a powerful and stirring story and will hopefully enable you to gain more insight into the conversations and to really grasp the depth and honesty shown by the young people. In the original transcript there is a significant gap between the two sections being used here but this is a way of enabling greater access to one very moving voice in the research. The transcript is followed by a short reflection on the text. These reflections are drawn from the transcript but have relevance within the totality of the data.

The participant, Suzi,[33] is 24 years old from an urban background in Scotland. She has an M.Sc and is currently studying for a Ph.D in a scientific discipline. She was part of a group of three female young adults, the other two participants being Lorna and Carrie.

The Transcript

S: when I was 14 I started to think about suicide. It had got too much. I had no one to talk to, no one to help me so in the end I decided to put a stop to it. I felt so low, so useless, mainly because I had been told that I was so many times.

Are you sure that you feel o.k. to talk about this?

S: It is hard in a way, I still get emotional about it, but it's fine. Carrie's heard about this before anyway. I've been told quite a few times that it helps to talk about it and it usually does. I've talked about it so much sometimes I forget that it's even me that this happened to. It all feels so unreal. I thought about it so much...at 14 dying isn't something that most people give much thought to. And even less people think about what ways they can kill themselves!

I have absolutely no idea why I decided it but I thought that hanging would be the best way. It would be instant and I wouldn't have to cut myself or anything like that. I set the whole thing up in the basement of the house on an evening when my family was out, rope and all. I didn't write a note or anything cause I figured they would know why, especially my stepmother. Anyway...there I was in my basement with everything arranged, standing on the chair and everything. I tried to put my head through the rope and I couldn't. Now you're probably thinking that I backed down, that I didn't really want to do it but that's not it. I was actually standing on this chair, trying to put my head through the loop and it literally wouldn't go through. I kept trying and honestly, I couldn't put my head through. I felt as though someone's hand was on the front of my head pushing against me so that I couldn't do it. It made no sense of course. I remember getting down and sitting on the seat for a while. I sat there thinking if I was doing something wrong, if I'd set the whole thing up. There was no space in my head for thoughts about what I was doing, was I doing the right thing or whatever. All I wanted was for this to work. Up I got and tried again and the same thing happened. I was just sitting on that seat looking across the room and this light appeared. I thought nothing of it but it got brighter and brighter until I was sure this wasn't anything to do with the electricity. I sat there a bit frightened really looking at this thing, not knowing what to think, and in the middle of it I appeared. It was like watching myself on T.V. or something...

C:...this sounds weird every time I hear it you know!

S: It feels weird explaining it too!! It was weird being there...I was literally sitting watching myself stand up on the chair, trying to put my head through the rope and not being able to. The whole picture was getting clearer and next I could see this hand resting on my forehead, not allowing my head to go through. It was so scary but...I don't know...amazing at the same time. I didn't know what to think....kind of still don't...

L: Did you get up and try again?

S: I did actually. That was how much I wanted it to work. I knew I wouldn't be able to this time though, I just knew inside it wouldn't work.

L: What happened to the light and your cinema screen?!S: Once I realised that there was a hand there stopping me, it just started to fade away. The basement didn't get darker or anything...I don't know how to explain it...it wasn't a light that brightened everything up, it was something that was there and almost kept its light inside...I don't know...

L: Are you making this up?

S: No way...I'd need to have some imagination to make this up! It really is what happened. It sounds crazy I know but honestly, I believe that God didn't want me to die, that there was a purpose for my life and this was the only way to stop me. That picture I saw, that was God's way of showing me that I wasn't going to be allowed to do it....maybe the hand on my head was actually happening, maybe an angel or something was stopping me, I don't know. The picture might have been a metaphor or something...God's way of explaining what was happening in a way that I could understand.

I can understand you not being able to share. It's a very personal experience. And moving. Who do you think you could have talked to about it? Where might you have gone?

S: I really don't know....I told a few friends but I was 15, I had as many questions, both personal and about what happened, as I had answers. I probably still do! I don't know where I could have gone...It would have been good to know that there was somewhere that I would be safe to talk about everything, to share all that was happening, and not have someone judge me, maybe not even try to fix things. People need space to talk about things without there being any judgement, where they can learn about other people's experiences in life and tell their own. They need to know that the people can be trusted, that people aren't going to walk out and blab. I suppose, because of what happened to me...I suppose the best place for me to go would have been to someone religious, like a minister or something, but I would never be able to do that. I don't know any ministers, so there's no way that I would talk to them...

Some Reflections[34]

Throughout the text Suzi shows awareness of other peoples reaction to her story. She tries to create an interest in her story and a warning that despite the dramatic nature of it, the story is nonetheless true. She is clearly aware of other people's cynicism and expresses strong empathy with the listener in recognition of the extraordinary nature of her story. However, at no point does Suzi doubt the reality of her experience nor will she allow people to impose a sensible or rationalistic interpretation upon it. This is not something that she has been prepared to do herself and the event has become so central to her sense of self that to accept the story is to accept Suzi herself.[35]

People process information in different ways and Suzi clearly does this cognitively. Perhaps the clearest example of this is that the whole process of her suicide was carefully planned and was set-up correctly. Although Suzi has difficulty with the expression of emotion, there is evidence of both mystery and uncertainty in her language. It is most significant that Suzi uses this type of language when she begins to reflect upon and interpret her experience.

As Suzi explains her experience it is apparent that cognitive approaches were simply not sufficient. Although she remains uncertain she is very clear that her experiences involve some revelation from God.

The suggestion is that Suzi not only had an experience but with it she developed a new method for processing information. This new method requires the use of different language, a language that describes some of the meanings and purpose in the experience and in Suzi's life. The experience in the basement was transformational, in that it not only saved her life, but also provided her with additional resources for understanding her life. Cognitive language - the core of Suzi's expression - is not capable of adequately explaining this transformational experience and so Suzi uses different language.

Although uncertainties still remain in her reflection, there are also a number of things that she is very clear about. She is adamant that the event involved a revelation from God, that God didn't allow her to die and that she was alive for a reason.

Throughout her story, and it would seem also her life, Suzi manages to hold onto the fact that the event occurred. She may not be entirely certain of its meaning, but she knows it means *something*. The truth of Suzi's story is that her friends ultimately accept the reality of her experience - even though it seems beyond belief and allied with the fact that Suzi doesn't have a full understanding or knowledge of the meaning of the incident. Suzi asks people to be open in the sharing with her and supporting her as she journeys, trying to find her way and a meaning that she can own.

This has implications for youth work, education and religion, as does the reaction of Lorna and Carrie. It is clear that Suzi's event is somewhat *weird*, a term Suzi uses to describe it. But it didn't need Suzi to make her event not *weird* for her friends to accept the truth of it. This final point raises additional questions about the attitudes, skills and motivations that someone like Suzi, and also her friends, require in each of us. Rather than imposing some meaning upon Suzi, for a person like her each of us needs an ability to listen, to share, to care and to create space so that others can hear, question, learn and grow to find the meanings that they desire.

To Continue....

Although there is a great deal more that could be drawn from this transcript - for instance, Suzi's understanding of God, her understanding of her experience, her expectations of religion, her needs to enable her to better self-reflect, her response to death, mystery, and fear - there is not space or need to do so here. There is much within the short text above that is evidenced within the whole of the data and would be best considered as a broad picture rather than only Suzi's individual story.

Suzi's story and the very short reflection illustrates some of the richness of the data and the honesty apparent in it. I hope as you read and consider the findings and recommendations in the following chapter, that you will be better able to hear beyond the analysis to the voices of the young people from which it is drawn.

[33] Her name, as with all the names in the fellowship, has been changed to maintain anonymity
[34] This part of the report is drawn from a presentation made by John Baxter-Brown and myself at the International Association for the Study of Youth Ministry Conference, January 2005.
[35] Although this is not necessarily a point of analysis, it is also important to recognise the affect that Suzi's self-perception and her story has on me as a participant in the conversation. Having read some of the text of the conversation you will hopefully have been able to observe some of the skills required in working with and researching young people. Suzi has not shared her story with many people and I had to be aware of her response to her own disclosure, as well as my response and that of the other people participating in the conversation.

Findings

The Unsaid

Before turning to the main areas of the findings, I wish to consider some of the things that might have been expected to arise in the conversations but which appeared rarely or in some cases not at all.

Throughout the conversations young people discussed religion and religious issues. Within these discussions there was very rarely any reference to religious celebrations e.g. Eid, Christmas, etc. This is particularly relevant because in recent years some towns and cities in the U.K. have had difficulty in presenting the Christian element of holidays like Christmas and this has been highly publicised through all the major media forms. During conversation about spirituality it would not necessarily have been anticipated that young people would mention these celebrations but with religion taking such a prominent place in the dialogue, it is more likely that they would have been discussed.

It is difficult to establish the reason for the omission of these celebrations from the conversations. Perhaps it is because these festivals do not feature highly in the lives of young people or that the religious foundation of them is not recognised. There is also some evidence that, at least in this area, the media may not be as influential in the lives of young people as generally assumed. This is a point I will discuss in more detail later. No matter the reason, it was a surprise that they did not feature more prominently.

Another surprising omission was the lack of discussion of horoscopes, the zodiac, reading your stars, tarot cards, fortune reading etc. I expected that this would have been mentioned as something relating to spirituality, especially among female young people. Young people may not treat reading the stars, fortune reading etc. with the greatest value, but on a number of occasions young people talked about being guided and knowing what they were meant to do. It is interesting that within these discussions about young peoples' future and destiny there does not seem to be a significant place for reading the stars, fortune reading etc.

Finally, within the data there are various mentions of a spiritual realm or spiritual world.

> *"I'm intrigued by peoples' spirits and I think there is a spiritual world that we don't see."*[36]

> Spirituality is, *"...related to believing in God and religion, that there's a spiritual world or something."*[37]

There are many young people who consider such a thing to exist but this does not appear to be a world of ghosts and ghouls as might be assumed. Ghosts and ghouls were actually never mentioned by young people, as least not in any conventional sense. Some young people do discuss instances of being guided by family or friends that have died and while these might be considered spirits, these instances do not make mention of any sort of visitation or sighting, or of ghosts.

Within conversation about spirits it would seem a natural progression for the subject of ghosts to enter the conversation. Although spirits were discussed these were not linked to ghosts, of places being haunted or of other things of this nature. I can only suggest that perhaps young people are considering terms like spiritual and spirituality more narrowly than first thought.

Understanding Language

It is clear in the data that there is some distinction between young peoples' understandings of words such as spirituality, spiritual, and spiritual experience, and the activities and thoughts taking place in life. Understandings and use of language does not necessarily reflect the thoughts, actions and feelings that are taking place in their lives. Taking Suzi as an example, there is uncertainty in her perception of herself as spiritual:

> "Mmm....Maybe...I think so...I'm not sure really....Yeah, probably....yeah"

yet she has the experience that is described in the text of her interview in the last chapter. There are many other examples of young people who have the most profound thoughts and feelings about a spiritual world, about God, faith, family, the world and who experience 'extraordinary events' yet they struggle to consider themselves to be spiritual or to express with any confidence their understanding of terms such as spiritual, spirituality or spiritual experience.

One of the key characteristics of young peoples' understanding is the high degree of uncertainty. There are most definitely some young people who are clear about their understandings and are at ease expressing this but in the main, responses were filled with don't knows and significant pauses for thought. This uncertainty is further evident in the wide variety of understandings expressed by young people:

> "I see it (spiritual) that there are two parts to every person. There is a part which is body and mind and stuff like that, but there is another part that is spiritual. It never dies. It's a part of the human that lives on. I don't know about heaven or reincarnation or anything like that, the religious things but I believe it goes on after we die."[38]

> "It's not an easy question to answer. I found it hard to answer

43

whether I was spiritual or not, maybe because I don't see it that way. There are angels and things like that, maybe there's a God too...there's a spiritual world connected to the one that we live in. Maybe I'm part of it, I don't know...there is something more than this world though.... " [39]

"Everyone is spiritual, everyone is created by God and has a desire to be close to God." [40]

"It's religion. People who go to church and believe in God are spiritual." [41]

"It made me think of something special...There's lots of people who believe in God but that doesn't make them spiritual. Maybe we are all spiritual in a way because we all think about God, if God exists or whatever. Maybe there's something in us that makes us think about things like that...I don't know...being spiritual just seems to me to be so much more than being religious." [42]

"I don't think there is a God like maybe the Christians believe in and definitely not like the Muslims think, but there might be something. Why can't we feel spiritual even if there isn't something more than what's in this world?" [43]

"...there is no such thing as spiritual. Everything is part of the world, what you can see and whatever..." [44]

As you will no doubt be able to see from the statements above, terms such as spiritual and spirituality have a wide and often conflicting variety of understandings among young people. On the one hand there are those who strongly connect these terms to religion while on the other hand there are those who suggest that people cannot be both spiritual and religious.

For some time I struggled to put these apparent conflicts together in any understandable way. I have come to the conclusion that regardless of exactly what relationship young people understand spirituality and religion to have, it is clear that one is being understood in relation to the other. Some young people set them one against the other, while others understand them to be synonymous. Even those who reject the notion of any such thing as spiritual, spirituality or otherness understand the language and do so with reference to religion.

> *"I don't think there is a God. I don't believe there is anything like a spiritual world or something outside this world...There is no God, nothing spiritual, nothing like that...I don't think most of religion is right. If people were right and God made the world then he did a crap job. That's reason enough to believe there is no God cause if there was then he would do a better job."* [45]

In previous research from people such as David Hay, it was shown that, "A few people see very little difference between religion and spirituality. Most make a clear distinction. Religion tends to be associated with what is publicly available, such as churches, mosques, Bibles, prayer books, religious officials, weddings and funerals....Spirituality is almost always seen as much warmer, associated with love, inspiration, wholeness, depth, mystery and personal devotions like prayer and meditation."[46]

There is still evidence of this separation of religion and spirituality as suggested by Hay and others. One example of this is the perception that a spiritual person is something special, it is something that very few people have ever been or that young people expect to be.

> *"I don't know but spiritual seems to me like it's something more than just religious...it's something special or something."* [47]

There are a number of other occurrences of young people stating that they believe there is a god or higher power or something and/or that they pray.[48] However, they are also very clear that they are not religious showing that this religion/spirituality divide is still observed by some young people.

"...when you asked about being spiritual, I thought you were meaning being religious, believing in God, that sort of thing, but I'm not religious. Spiritual is about how I see the world, how I experience life. We can all be spiritual if we choose to be, we can be connected to things, people, places. We can feel a strong bond, something different and special about it." [49]

"(spirituality)...doesn't have anything to do with religion. It's more about me, myself and the world... It's not about God or anything like that. Having the soil in my hands, in a way it's like having the earth's soul in my hand. The earth doesn't judge me. It gives me such a feeling of peace. I often sit and talk to the earth or trees or sky. I feel connected to the whole of existence, to all the earth. It can be such a peaceful time. I can be so free with the earth, try to experience all of me. I will sometimes sit and look into the soil or into water and look at it for ages, and feel so much of the world, so much peace and contentedness." [50]

From work such as that by David Hay it was said that the majority of people held to the separation of religion and spirituality and that a few understood them as having very little difference. However the conversations that I engaged in show a significant increase in the idea that there is little difference in religion and spirituality. When asked the two set questions the vast majority of young people began to talk about religion and to express their understanding as some of the following:

"It's all the same to me...spiritual, religious, it's all the same." [51]

"Going to church and praying and believing in God, that's what spiritual is." [52]

"Spiritual is just to do with religion. People who are religious, they think that they are spiritual." [53]

"I would say people who go to church or follow a religion should be spiritual." [54]

It is true that young people who described themselves as Christian or religious understood spiritual and religious to be connected i.e. they went to church or believed in God therefore they were spiritual. But the vast majority of young people with whom I spoke were not involved in religion and they too understood religious and spiritual to be synonymous.

This may be evidence of a significant cultural shift. It is the case that people in the 1960s and '70s in particular began to move away from the mainstream religions towards what was called spirituality. This separation has pervaded mainstream thinking but perhaps the current generation and those to follow will no longer see this separation as valid. This area would obviously require further investigation especially among young people and older children. It does appear though, that the religious/spiritual divide is no longer as stark or significant as it may previously have been.

A particular issue with this renewed understanding and use of language lies in young peoples' largely negative attitude to religion.[55] As there is a shift towards identifying spiritual with religious so it is likely that young people will become negative towards any and all things spiritual. If this understanding increases then in time young people are probably going to become negatively disposed to consideration of spiritual, spirituality, soul, god, heaven, angels etc. Not only will young people be 'switched off' to religion but in time they may also become antagonistic towards any language that is connected with it.

Of course it could be argued that the more positive attitude to spiritual language will improve perceptions towards religion but I don't see any reason why this would be the case. As you will see, the negative attitude to religious institutions is so strong that it is highly unlikely that the slightly more positive attitude to spirituality will become the driving force – as identification between the spiritual and the religious increases.

It is significant that quite a number of young people suggested that terms like spiritual and spirituality are already not a feature in their day-to-day language.

> *"..spiritual...To be honest, it's a word I would never think of using."* [56]

> *"I've never thought about these things much, and I've certainly never talked about it!"* [57]

While I am certain that this is due in part to the uncertainty of understanding, this probably also has much to do with the apparent alienation from religion that is already felt by many young people. Indeed some of the language is already considered religious e.g.

> *"Soul seems religious somehow...Soul really does sound religious, the same way spiritual does."* [58]

If young people already understand spirituality and religion to be closely linked, and they are negatively inclined towards religion, then in time they are also going to be negatively inclined towards terms like spiritual and spirituality.

Having said that, it is very important to recognise that no young person ever declined to take part in the conversations and were able to fully engage once the process began. Many young people suggested that they weren't spiritual or had never talked about such things, but when in conversation with these same young people something 'buried' came to the fore. No one declined to participate and when they did, every person had much to offer to the conversation.

My view is that this openness came about mainly because of the process that was used. Although each individual may have had an uncertainty in understanding and when often there was no consensus of meaning among a group of friends, each person was still able to enter their understanding and use of language into the conversation. At no time was anyone left to feel that they were incorrect or that they had to accept a certain meaning of spiritual, spirituality or even God, angels or prayer but the process did encourage them to consider and reflect on their own and other peoples' use of language and on their understandings. The methodology that was used has a lot to offer in encouraging young people to reflect and perhaps bring some greater clarity to their understandings and experiences. In a sense, the process encouraged each person to reflect on those things that had been 'buried' and to make them public so that others may reflect on them.

Another significant point here is that at the end of the conversations young people expressed appreciation of the space that had been created for them.

> *"Thanks for talking to us. I was dead apprehensive at the start, didn't know what was going to happen but I've really enjoyed it."* [59]

> *"Yeah, thank you. It's not often people would approach us in the street, maybe if we didn't wear black they might! I found the conversation good, it's great to talk to someone who really is interested and is respectful of what we are saying. That doesn't happen very often."* [60]

> *"Thanks for talking to us. It's good to have a chance to talk about who you are, what you think, without having someone judging you or wanting to change you."* [61]

But for some this went even further:

> *"You've given me a lot to think about. Made me wonder if there is a God or something out there after all. Might have to reconsider everything!"* [62]

"I liked your question about what God is not. That's something I will think about a lot...maybe that way I might actually find God. I'd love to have a place to go to think these things through, to talk about them and hear from others. That's something else I will look for I think....thank you for talking to me. I have enjoyed it a lot. I wish more people would talk and listen like you have with us. Maybe that's how I will search...by going up to people in pubs and coffee shops and asking them questions like you have....that would be scary but I bet I would learn so much about life and about myself too." [63]

"You've given me lots to think about. It's funny 'cause I feel kind of encouraged to go out and try new things, you know, to help people and look after the world like I should. And you weren't even trying to do that!" [64]

"You've made me realise that the thing I need most in life is to find God." [65]

My view is that the key aspect in all this is that young people are interested and do consider spiritual/religious issues. Some even have very extraordinary 'spiritual' experiences. There is clear evidence of something 'buried' among young people, something that they know about but don't often have the opportunity to reflect upon. They may have uncertainties about language and about experiences but the way to engage with this is not to tell them what things mean or what you believe, but rather just to walk with them as they search for their meanings. In effect we would be journeying and searching along with them. By doing this not only are young people likely to remain interested in spiritual/religious language and issues and develop stronger understandings, they may even find some meaning in their search.

Reaction to Religion

As I have already explained, young people generally relate terms like spiritual, spirituality and religion very closely. This association meant that a considerable portion of each conversation focussed on religion. The U.K., and England in particular is considered multi-cultural so I was surprised that when young people discussed religion, God etc. they almost exclusively talked about Christianity or in Christian terms.

"People who are religious, who go to church, they'd think that they are spiritual." [66]

"Spiritual people are Christians, people who go to church and are religious.." [67]

"...Jesus is the Son of God and rose from the dead. They talk about sin too..." [68]

Although the young people I engaged with referred firstly to Christianity, other religions were mentioned on a few occasions and it did not appear to be the case that young people valued one religion over another. For instance:

"I'm not like Buddha or Jesus...." [69]

"All the religions are the same. They believe some different things but they all have the same sort of god. If it's Islam, Christianity, Judaism, whatever, it's all the same god. They are all the same to me." [70]

"People who go to a mosque or to church, it's all the same really. Religious, spiritual, it's all the same to me. ...they all say prayers and try to connect to God." [71]

The Hare Krishnas, "...I'd always just think of them as religious too. Different religious but still religious...They look funny in orange and their hair all cut..." [72]

Yet these other faiths were mentioned infrequently and it was only Christianity that they talked of in great detail. They didn't necessarily have some association with any aspect of Christianity but they do have definite feelings, understandings and opinions about it. This is probably similar to the last census when 71.9% of people defined themselves as Christians. Although people may not consider themselves religious, when asked about their religion or even just religion in general, it is Christianity that is thought of.

For that reason, in the remainder of this section, unless it is specifically stated otherwise, when religion is discussed it is only in reference to Christianity and the church. If other religions or faiths are being considered, then they will be specifically referenced.

For some readers the area of religion may be a sensitive one and therefore my effort to express young peoples' reaction to and thoughts and feelings about religion have taken a considerable amount of time. The reality is that young people had a great deal to say, most of it expressed very passionately and in the main their thoughts and feelings were not positive. Frankly, they were quite the opposite. When so many young people respond in the same fashion there is little option but to sit up and take notice.

"Religion has been such a negative force in the world. I believe there's a God, but I'd never go to church again. Christians only make it harder to see God, to experience things. Christianity puts such a load of shit around God...." [73]

"Religion is such a load of shit." [74]

"I used to go to church but I stopped when I was about ten. I didn't stop believing in God but really, what's Adam and Eve got to do with my life? You get told all these stories that are kind of interesting but they get surrounded with all this other crap. It's as if every story in the Bible has to have some great 'don't do that' kind of message. If people were allowed to read and think for themselves, younger people

especially, then maybe the whole thing wouldn't seem so shit." [75]

"People go to church and hear some man talking and telling them what the Bible says. Well I can read it for myself if I want, I don't need someone telling me what's right or how to act. Sometime I would love to see someone just put their hand up and ask the guy what the hell he's talking about. Not being able to ask questions or say how you feel about stuff, it's so shit." [76]

"It's like going to a concert. If it's shit then I am going to get up and leave and it's like that with religion. It's rubbish so I don't go. I do believe there is something, God or something, but I'm not Christian. Sometimes I even pray but I'd never want to sit in church or stuff like that." [77]

"God gets such a bad press because of all the shit that religious people do, like all the gay stuff and women priests..." [78]

So many young people stated that religion, the Church, Christianity and/or Christians were 'shit' that it was something I could not fail to miss. There were of course many other things that were said. For instance, rather than concluding that the Church is shit, perhaps I could conclude that it's boring.

"If Jesus is who he is supposed to be, God or whatever, then Christians shouldn't be all boring like they are. They should be happy and out helping people, the poor and homeless." [79]

"I feel like the Christian life is so boring and doesn't really make much difference in the world. You know, if Jesus said to give your money to the poor then every Christian should do it. They should do all that the Bible says or none of it, not just the bits that suit them." [80]

Or people are hypocritical....

"Christians dress fancy on Sunday and act all close to God and

everything but come Monday they lie and cheat and rip you off...The Christians I know just do whatever they like and then tell you about God. They're complete shite." [81]

"Christians are liars. They are always saying one thing and doing another...if people believe stuff and keep telling you that you should be Christian too, then they should live like it matters...They should be doing good to people. They should be doing what they say and what it says in the Bible." [82]

Or false...

"...have you ever seen what they do? Clapping and putting their hands in the air. I remember watching a video of that stuff in school. Now that was weird! It all seemed so false. I've only seen stuff like that at big concerts or maybe a football match or something. It's dead creepy! I'm sure that they would say that they are worshipping God. I don't get it though. It all seems so unnatural, so unreal. Never mind all the hands in the air, even the singing doesn't seem real. It's all put on but I don't know why anyone would." [83]

"They're so false, all singing and praying and smiling. It's meaningless, totally false. Like they could sing all happy and the rest of the world can die or something" [84]

Or it's irrelevant...

"I used to go to church but stopped when I was about 10...that was fine when you are a young kid but when you get older it seemed pretty irrelevant to the rest of life I suppose." [85]

"Irrelevant is a good word. When I was young I hated being sent to church but I quite enjoyed it when I got there. I liked drawing and the stories, stuff like that. What child doesn't?! But when I was maybe 10 or so, the whole thing seemed such a big waste of time. That's why I said irrelevant is a good description. Honestly, when

anyone gets to 11, 12, 13, what has Noah or Moses got to do with anything?! I'm not even sure that people who keep going really want to be there. I haven't been for years, but I'd still see church on TV the odd time and it looks the same. No one ever looks like they want to be there... [86]

Or it doesn't change anything...

"Church is too much about being seen there and about doing all the right things. It's not about growing or being challenged or changing. Church allows people to stay as they are and not have to really put their beliefs into practice." [87]

Or it controls people...

"I no longer feel that the traditional religions, including Christianity, are the best way to grow as a person, as a spiritual person. There isn't the freedom to express yourself, to find your own way to communicate with God. There are too many expectations on people..." [88]

"I want to decide how I feel about God and the Bible or whatever, about what's good and bad for me, but church doesn't let you do that." [89]

Or it tells people what to believe rather than helping them to know God....

"Church is more about services and priests telling you what to believe about God and Jesus than it is about giving you a safe space to search your own heart and soul." [90]

"...there isn't space in any church I have been in to wonder about things...to consider things fully...there just seems to be nowhere, no church at least, that people talk and think about things in life.....I've a younger sister, she's 14 now and where can she go to ask questions,

to wonder if there is a God or if the Bible is true. Or what prayer is for. People are brought up to accept things and the place they should be considering things, religious questions I suppose, the place they should be asking about these things is in church but I don't know any church where people do." [91]

"Religion is man wrapping whatever higher power there is, it's covering it up with all this jargon, and rules and contradictions. Instead of it being something that everyone can and should experience it becomes something that people argue over..." [92]

Or it's just about following rules....

"...it's just following a load of shit rules. It doesn't make any difference in the world." [93]

"I always feel that there are rules to follow, the right things to do or say to fit in.

What sort of rules?

Oh just the normal stuff....don't drink, don't swear, don't have sex, go to church....you shouldn't be in bars or night clubs....I don't know...it seems like there are all these things that people expect you to be." [94]

Or it's judgemental

"People in church just want to judge you. They're no better than anyone else but they always act like they are." [95]

But on their own none of those options really convey the whole truth. The fact of the matter is that so many young people said that church is shit that it is simply impossible to ignore.

The vast majority of young people do view the Church as

irrelevant, controlling etc. but it is the 'shit' description that seems to combine these negative observations. It also does more than this. The use of the word 'shit' holds much more meaning than just boring, irrelevant etc. It's passionate. It's aggressive. It's caring because it is most certainly not indifferent.

The best way I can explain this is with reference to the comedian Billy Connelly. His use of language has greater depth than only the dictionary meaning of each word. Each word is given greater meaning because of how he uses it. It is not just what he says that is important but also how he says it. It is this type of depth that is contained in young peoples' description of the Church as 'shit'.

Of course not every young person marked religion in this way. I did talk with a number of young people who were church attendees, or had been previously, and they presented some positive aspects of religion.

"I used to go to church....it could be kind of interesting. I like some of the stories about all the wars and kings and things..." [96]

"I enjoy the singing and worship in some places and the prayers in communion in other places" [97]

There were also some positive responses by young people who were not church attendees and who would not describe themselves as spiritual. These however were quite rare:

"I love the liturgy and some of the religious aspects of church..." [98]

"All the prayers and songs, the stuff about God being good and planning things, it was interesting to hear. I wasn't bored. I can only say it was irrelevant maybe. If I was doing that every week than I reckon I would be bored." [99]

Having said all that, even in the few cases when religion was reacted to more positively, it was still tempered with some negativity or at least a desire to see something better.

> *"I used to go to church....it could be kind of interesting. I like some of the stories about all the wars and kings and things but honestly, if I hadn't heard them it wouldn't matter. It would have been like not doing some history at school. It wouldn't matter if I didn't know. Like Joseph...what's some guy in a coloured coat to do with anything?"* [100]

> *"I've heard so many stories and have a few negative experiences myself. I'd have to work through those really. I love the liturgy and some of the religious aspects of the Church but I'd have to be part of a freer Church, a place where space was given to think and feel and learn...I want the freedom to choose and to think for myself."* [101]

> *"Church is good though...it's somewhere that people should go but...I feel like church should be much more than it is, it should provide more for people, especially young people. When people are young they are questioning so many things and accepting things too and Church should be somewhere that they can go to talk and consider things. Anyone I know that does go to church, I feel like sometimes they are willing to accept things to easily."* [102]

I hope that what I have written thus far has shown the depth of feeling among young people about religion. It is generally accepted that the Church has problems and has been declining in numbers for quite some time. Those ultimately responsible for young peoples' reaction to religion are those attending or supporting the institutions and in order to respond to the current situation something of the reasons behind young peoples' angry reaction needs to be understood. Following the interactions with young people, I have reached the conclusion that the foundation of the reaction comes down to one or both of the following:

Perception: It could well be the case that young people have not experienced or do not know about 'real' religion. Perhaps their observation of religion is an unfounded view that is drawn from a poor representation of religion in movies, television, education, books, newspapers etc. It was recently suggested to me that young people think as they do because of television shows like the Vicar of Dibley. While my personal view is that there is probably some truth in this idea, the conversations that I had with young people do not generally support this argument. I was somewhat surprised that when I asked young people where they thought their feelings about religion came from they rarely referred to the generally assumed sources of television, movies, internet and magazines. There were of course a small number of others who do appear do be drawing from these sources:

"S: That's one of the things people in church have got right, they hate queers too. They won't let them into church and they never should. Almost seems like a good reason to go to church!!

What's the problem with gay people?

S: Its fuckin' wrong. It's just disgusting. It's totally against everything that's right. Have you ever seen two queers kissing or anything? It turns my stomach.

And you feel the same John?

J: Yeah course I do. It's wrong what they do. It's in the Bible. That's why Christians hate them too. It's been all in the news and everything. We should go back to the old days when people had to believe in God and if you were a witch or queer or whatever you got burned at the stake.

Do you feel the same for men and women?

J: Nah not really. Men should be killed but some women are ok, but only some. The big butch lesbians are just like men but some of the pretty lessies, they're ok. They're good to watch and look at so that's ok. Men are fucking disgusting.

S: Yeah lessies are ok but men, they deserve a good kicking.

John, you said that you know there is a God. If you knew that a gay person believed in God would it make any difference?

J: No of course not. Why should it? Shit, God hates gays too doesn't He! The Bible says so. It's near the start but there is something about stoning men who do stuff with men. That's what I think we should do with them. It doesn't matter whether they believe in God or not.

S: I don't know if there is a God, I think there probably is but he wouldn't be protecting queers. Life here is not exactly good so its not like God really gives a shit anyway." [103]

From the text above I would suggest that these two young men are drawing on a number of sources, even if they are not aware of them. They make mention of this story being in the news and are obviously aware of gathering information from those sources, but there also seems to be a deeper knowledge, John stating that God's *hatred* of gay people is near the start of the Bible. Perhaps he also drew this information from newspapers or television news but I think that it is more likely he has gathered these details from some other unidentified source.

I use this particular situation to also illustrate that some of the reactions young people have to religion are because they have not experienced or do not know about religion. Some of the reaction to religion among young people may be similar to this, being drawn from false or incomplete information. For the two young men above, their perception of the Church is *their* reality, but I doubt very much that most churchgoers would accept their ideas as the *actual* reality. I can only hope that their reactions are drawn from unfounded observations that draw on a poor representation of religion but, either way, their view of religion should be enough to make any follower of religion concerned about young peoples' perceptions.

Content: As I explained before, young people did not generally suggest that their reaction to religion was drawn from television, newspapers, movies etc. but there was a regularly suggested point of reference, that of religious education.

> *"I haven't done any religion since I left school. I guess anything that I know I got in R.E. in school or maybe a bit from assemblies or something."* [104]

> *"The only things I know about church I heard in R.E. when I was at school."* [105]

> *"Only place I've done anything about religion was in R.E. class I suppose, but that teaches you about different religions. I never remember talking about what God might be like or even if the different religions are right or anything. It was more Christians do this, Muslims do this, that sort of thing. It would have been far more interesting to have been able to think about things like that, stead of being taught some crap about how this church works and looks like inside."* [106]

Although there were some positive responses to the role of Religious Education:

> *"I only know what I was taught in R.E. I've never read the Bible or Koran. I remember about Noah and the whole creation story. I remember learning about the commandments...you shouldn't steal or kill. It was interesting..."* [107]

> *"What is taught in school is taught like it is fact and kids are all supposed to accept it. I know I did. It isn't all fact though. History for example is taught like fact but the point of history is that it can*

be disputed. Perhaps R.E. is actually the only honest subject in school because it doesn't teach everything as fact. It gives options and tells you what different religions say and then you can go and make up your own mind." [108]

"I suppose I learned something about other religions that I wouldn't have known. I don't really know any religious people so I would have no way to learn about Jews or Muslims, or even Christians if I didn't have R.E." [109]

the responses were generally negative:

"The only time I can remember anything to do with religion was in R.E. class at school and I couldn't tell you one thing that I was taught." [110]

"...no one takes it seriously because it's not the same as all the other subjects... if school is always going to pretend that its about facts then maybe R.E. shouldn't be taught there because it doesn't fit in. It's good that it doesn't fit but people don't listen because they know its not fact and you don't have to do exams. Kids are made to believe that every thing else in school is fact. They aren't taught to think and make up their own minds. People just don't listen in R.E." [111]

"R.E. at school...Oh my God!" [112]

Regardless of young peoples' feelings about Religion Education, it does appear to be the main source of information about religion. This being the case, it must be admitted that the information they will be given will be correct. For instance, young people aren't taught that Judaism has two commandments which are, 'Eat, drink and be merry' and 'Never go to school.' They are presented with information that is factually correct and for that reason it must be accepted that young people do know something about the content of various religions.

While some young people may understand only a little and consequently perceive religion wrongly, there are others who clearly know it more deeply:

> *"I enjoy the singing in some places, and the prayers and communion in other places..."* [113]

> *"I remember things from when I was at Sunday school and I've no reason to doubt them I suppose...in the Bible he is meant to have healed people and fed the 5000 and...he is said to have risen from the dead."* [114]

While misguided perceptions do play a part in young peoples' reactions to religion, it is only half the story. It is simply not feasible to take young peoples' positive reactions to religion and say that they are right, while totally rejecting the validity of other young peoples' negative reactions as just perception. The really pertinent question is, how often do young people have to say that Church is shit before it is accepted that what they say is the truth? While some of the negativity is due to misconceptions e.g. the two young mens' understanding of gay people and the Church, some of the negativity surely also comes because young peoples' understanding of religion is actually correct.

In consideration of these 'correct understandings', young people rarely commented on the church building or the worship. Neither did they regularly say that church was boring. The issues young people raised were more often concerned with showing love, being free to question and to decide for yourself, having some control of activities, of being respected, of being emotionally safe etc. As you will hopefully see in the next section, young people consistently expressed a desire for a safe place where they can reflect, both alone and in conjunction with others, but felt that the church was not this place.

While I am sure some will want to say that their church is like that, other researchers have also observed that "...it is much more common to hear members of congregations say, 'I was saddened to learn' than 'I was furious', or 'It was a humbling experience' than 'I felt proud'. It is rare to hear people speak openly in this setting about the full range of their emotions. Generally speaking, that which one should be tends to be given more prominence in the congregational domain than that which one is."[115] Reflecting again on the example of Suzi from the last chapter, if young people like her are correct and at least some aspects of religion are shit then the question has to be, how can the environment and culture be created to support and encourage Suzi to find the meaning and purpose of the extraordinary event in her life, without resorting to just telling her it was God? As one young person commented,

> *"It seems so stupid that church is supposed to be about God and Christians aren't meant to drink but I'm sitting in a pub talking more about God than I ever have in church!"* [116]

Without question, the most positive factor to be drawn from what young people had to say is that they care and are interested. I recently heard it said that the opposite of love isn't hate, it's indifference. This is very fitting when considering young people and religion because although they may be negatively disposed, at least they think and feel something. If they didn't care they wouldn't have such strong responses. Young people expect religion, Christians and the Church to be something and their expectations are not being met. Indeed, it would seem that it's not even close!

In the first section of this chapter I explained how young people seem to understand terms like spiritual, spiritual experience, religion and spirituality. I expressed young peoples' close association of all these terms, and how there is also a high degree of uncertainty and a wide range of understandings. In this section I intend to outline many of the things that young people discussed in our conversations and from that to express what I believe to be an understanding of spiritual, spirituality and spiritual experience that unites all these things.

Spiritual Experiences

I turn first to this complex area because there has already been strong evidence of it in Suzi's text from the last chapter. She was far from being the only person who experienced an event such as that:

- Louise who said that she wasn't spiritual but chose her university course because,

"I just knew inside that law is the path for me." [117]

- Paul described an event in his life at a Christian conference,

"I enjoy going to worship at big conferences and meetings. I love the power there is in so many people worshipping God. I often feel the Holy Spirit at these meetings but one time in particular always moves me. I don't often do this but I went to the front for prayer. It was such a special time for me. I stood at the front with all these people beside me and everyone else singing from behind. It seemed like there were millions singing! This guy was praying for me with his hand on my head. I didn't fall over or anything but I felt this ache in my belly, this real heat. I wasn't hot though, I wasn't sweating or anything, I just felt this thing inside, this power or presence or something. I was so happy, but happy doesn't even describe. I wanted to go nuts cause I felt so peaceful, so right, so excited. It's the most amazing feeling I have ever had...even better than sex and that's hard to beat!" [118]

- When Chris was asked if he'd ever experienced anything extraordinary he replied,

"Yeah, loads! The biggest one for me was when my gran was ill. The doctors told her that she was going to die in a week or so. I had been

praying for her, but I wanted to try some magic...It was crazy to watch her get better everyday, each day she improved that bit more until within the week she was up walking around the hospital instead of dying. She left the hospital 9 days after I started the spell. It was such a feeling to know that I helped to do that...I know that magic doesn't always work so there was always this thing in my mind that it wouldn't work. The doctor told her she would die so she probably would. I was sure I would do something wrong. I'm certain now that I helped to save her but I know it won't always work." [119]

Many young people have events ranging from making choices because of feelings of peace and easiness, through to some of the more extraordinary or miraculous events like those above. Even though I have called this aspect 'spiritual experience', I am somewhat apprehensive about doing so because so few young people actually name their events in this way. It is often argued that young people don't have a language to express their experiences, and many other events in their lives. However there is great controversy over what constitutes an experience, never mind a 'religious', 'transcendent' or 'spiritual' experience and I have come to realise how difficult language also is for adults!

It would appear that I am like most young people as I struggle to find the language to name these events but I have chosen to label them spiritual experiences. This is clearly difficult because I am not in a position to decide which experiences are included and which are not. To do this is to fall into the trap that David Hay warns of: "...In a multi-faith and highly secularised nation such as Britain, the spirituality of most people is liable to be overlooked." [120] so I have endeavoured to be as broad and open as possible.

Having said all that, I am not certain that naming the event is as important or useful as understanding the reason behind it. Taking again the example of Suzi, throughout her story, and it would seem also her life, Suzi manages to hold onto the fact that her event actually occurred. She may not yet know what it means, but she seems certain that it means something. And herein lies the problem.... If we are honest, how many of us would not spend time 'telling' Suzi that her event was from God or that it means x, y or z? How many of us would not spend time directing her one way or another? While conversing and journeying with Suzi we may be able to offer her some suggestions and although it might seem much easier to turn to Suzi and tell her that her event was a spiritual experience, it was God or it was this or that, we are not in a position to make such a judgement. We were not there and we did not experience Suzi's event and even more than that, this type of judgement is not what Suzi asks for.

Suzi retains the *fact* that her experience occurred and the belief that it means something, even though she remains uncertain what this meaning is. Despite not having a full understanding of the event and that it seems beyond belief, her friends ultimately accept the reality of the event. Alongside this acceptance Suzi asks each one of us to be more open in sharing with her and supporting her as she journeys, trying to find her way, trying to find a meaning that she can own, trying to better understand that which is buried within.

> *"It would have been good to know that there was somewhere that I would be safe to talk about everything, to share all that was happening, and not have someone judge me, maybe not even try to fix things. People need space to talk about things without there being any judgement, where they can learn about other people's experiences in life and tell their own. They need to know that the people can be trusted, that people aren't going to walk out and blab. I suppose, because of what happened to me...I suppose the best place for me to go would have been to someone religious, like a minister or something, but I would never be able to do that. I don't know any ministers, so there's no way that I would talk to them..."* [121]

Prayer

In some way similar to using the phrase 'spiritual experiences' to describe activities in the lives of young people, I have some reservations about using the term 'prayer'. Although some young people do use this term to describe this activity, it does not always follow traditional understandings and to only consider it in this way is to not see the whole picture. Although many young people are communicating with something outside of themselves, they are generally not using prayer in a religious sense or with religion in mind.

> *"I know I have to make my own way in the world, but I do talk a lot to the spirit as a guide. I know the spirit wants me to be all I can be, to grow and learn and experience, so I am always chatting away. It's prayer in a way, but it's not like they do in religion. I pray as I walk, or run or whenever I want. I don't have to do anything fancy or follow a ritual. I chat away to my friend and helper the spirit."* [122]

> *"People can communicate with everything, trees, plants, everything. Anyone can do it and we should all be trying."* [123]

The perceived disconnection from religion does not in anyway diminish the importance of this activity for young people. For many it is a vital and regular activity.

> *"It is important to pray about things but it's not easy to do it all the time."* [124]

> *"I try to every day. It's important to try but I know I don't do it as much as I should...Praying is so important...if you feel the spirit close it makes doing the right thing, creating the right thing so much easier."* [125]

Like with most aspects of spirituality among young people, there is not a generally accepted consensus. Young people are as likely to pray, as they are to be critical of others who pray.

"I've always felt that instead of saying prayers and asking God to help, maybe people should do more to help themselves and others. Praying that God will...I don't know...take care of old people or something, or feed people in a famine....the people should go and feed the others in a famine instead of saying prayers. People use prayers so that they feel better and don't have to go and do anything".[126]

It is obvious that young people pray in a variety of ways and for a variety of reasons and there are also some young people who value prayer even though they themselves rarely or never pray. In one particularly powerful story Danielle explained how the Salvation Army had approached her when she was homeless:[127]

"I became comfortable with a few of them I suppose, one girl in particular. I started asking them why they did this stuff, why they were out in the freezing cold when they had no need to be. I got to know them so I could talk to them a bit more personally, tell them things that had happened, and they gave me some advice and always said that they prayed for me. That was weird for me, but well, it wasn't doing me any harm so it didn't matter whether they did or not. When I was homeless I tended to sleep in different places rather than one spot. I always thought that it would be safer, I'd be harder to find that way. But I always slept near other people cause I suppose I thought there would be safety in numbers. Well, this one night I was sleeping near 6 other people, under this bridge. We all slept very close, to keep warm and dry. That night 4 guys came to where we were sleeping and stole everything off the other 6 people, everything. They took their clothes and what little food and money that was there. For some reason they never touched me. At first I thought maybe it was cause I was a woman but 2 of the other people were women too. I was shocked. And sad for the others too of course. It was so odd. The other guys said it was as if I was invisible. I was lying so still but the other guys said it was obvious I was there. They could see my face and hands under the blanket that I had and the muggers walked past me numerous times. They couldn't have missed me. I told the Salvation Army people about it and it turned out that the girl I was friendly with, her and her husband pray at midnight or so every

night, before they go to bed. They were praying for me at the time everyone else was being mugged and robbed. It could be just coincidence or that I wasn't seen but I find that so hard to believe. I really love the idea that these guys couldn't see me, that I was invisible or something!"

She went on to say that

"I'm still not religious, I don't go to Church or anything, and I'm not sure if there is a God, but I do believe the prayers did something. I think that at least, each person is connected in some way. We can influence each other and care for each other physically and spiritually...I think people can connect in that way...with a person who is so in tune with their spirit, with everything about them."

This also illustrates the point that young people are not necessarily considering prayer in traditional ways, but they do value the activity. Danielle values prayer even though she may not pray but there are other young people that perceive 'prayers' being used as a 'crutch' or a 'therapist'.

"I think a lot of religious people turn to God as a crutch, as something they use to make the world seem better or to pray so that this God out there will help them with things." [128]

"People have problems and need help so they turn to God, who isn't actually there. There was a communist guy who said religion was a drug for people, something to keep them happy." [129]

There are certainly aspects of this in young peoples' prayer, with some people quite clear that prayer makes them feel good and at ease:

"It did make me feel better, not so nervous, maybe that I wasn't on my own. It there is a God, prayer would be a good way to talk to him." [130]

"If I think of someone I would usually say a quick prayer that God would keep them safe but most of the time I'd probably only pray when I need help with something or I'm feeling a bit low. Kind of like a problem shared is a problem halved I guess." [131]

but these very same young people also see something greater in their use of prayer;

"But we need to listen too and not many people do that. The world might be a whole lot different place if people knew how to listen to God." [132]

"I know people would probably think I'm stupid to pray like I do. It makes me feel better course it does but it does something too. It changes things. I know when I am praying that I'm feeling different but I know there are people who are helped at exactly the time I pray. Its not just coincidence. If people took the time to pray - and to act too - but even just to pray, the world would be a different place." [133]

The 'crutch' idea though is not the sole reason that young people pray. By praying young people are often using God, a spirit, or 'something' as a confidante, as someone/something to be trusted.

"I know I can say whatever I want in my heart. Is there a God or whatever out there? Well who knows but it really helps me to share things with whatever is out there. Sometimes I try to talk to family that have died, my grandparents especially. I always liked spending time with them when they were here, so I've just kept sharing stuff with them even though I can't see them." [134]

"Its easy to talk to God. No matter what's going on or what you say, I know he's not going to tell anyone. He can't. So I can say whatever I like. I remember some nights when things have been really tough that I have been shouting and swearing, but only in my mind of course. It's my communication with something I can trust." [135]

71

While I do not wish to devalue this activity in any way, I think that using prayer in this way says much about the relationships available to young people. There are of course young people who both pray and have beneficial relationships but I wonder if other young people were offered something of the spaces and opportunities requested by Suzi among others, would they continue to communicate with something unknown? I wonder if some young people are using prayer because they don't have the confidence in people?

Prayers are being made to 'something' that young people have often not experienced. Many young people pray more in the hope that there might be something out there than because of any belief that there is a God or spirit. It's a case of 'roll the dice and hope' and I think young people may gain more by having trusted relationships in safe spaces where real issues could be shared rather than hoping that something that *might* be out there *might* help them.

There is some communication occurring between many young people and a spirit, God or something but a balance needs to be achieved where 'physical' people can listen, support and help young people in daily life without diminishing the communication with an 'unphysical' being. The support that young people request could easily be provided while maintaining the role of prayer in their life but within that process young people should be encouraged to reflect on what they are doing. If there is no value in this prayer activity then reflection will ultimately bring this to light. Of course the opposite is also true. If young people reflect on their actions and the outcomes of these actions, then praying could well become something even more valuable.

Another important aspect of prayer is listening. This is an important aspect of 'human' relationships for young people but it is also part of 'non-human' relationships. Prayer for many young people is focussed on asking for things for both yourself and others, but some young people use it as a form of guidance.

"Sometimes I will sit in my room and pray. Sometimes I will go for a walk, or maybe I will go out somewhere and sit in the air. Some days I go to a coffee shop....just anything that allows me to relax and try to let out whatever is inside, and hear whatever is on the outside."
136

"I don't think I would call it prayer cause I don't really say much but I do try to listen. I want God, my spirit, my heart or whatever is to guide me, to keep me safe and help me make the best choices for life."
137

They are eager to hear what God, the spirit etc. has to say to them but, when considering prayer, it is interesting to note that young people also often request space to reflect and to be listened to. As important as prayer may be in the life of quite a number of young people, it is very significant that they try to listen to a 'non-human' presence yet complain of not being listened to by other people. Whether positively or negatively, providing these 'human' relationships will surely affect prayer among young people but we should doubtless be making every effort to create the relationships and spaces that young people are seeking.

Understanding Spirituality: A Diversity of Views?

From the previous sections it is clear that there is much occurring in the life of young people that might be considered spirituality. It is also clear that there is much disparity and uncertainty about what these experiences mean and how they, and the language surrounding them, are understood. This section is an attempt to throw some light on this difficult area.

As I waded through the mountain of available data I was often excited but was also often frustrated. On the one hand there would be one young person who would say there is no such thing as spiritual or spirituality but then they would discuss these topics for an hour and also show a great deal of evidence in their life of spirituality, as it might be traditionally understood. On the other hand there are young people who are adamant that there are such things as spirituality or something spiritual, but then say they don't know what it is and have never experienced it.

Young people obviously understand and experience things differently but it was clear in the development of theory that there was something in common. All the thoughts, feelings, experiences and ideas were connected but it was proving difficult to clarify this. Working on this data it became difficult, 'to see the wood for the trees.' That was until I met a 24-year-old young man in a pub in Northern Ireland. He was enquiring about my work, as many people do, and rather than go into a boring explanation I asked him whether I could ask him and the friend who was with him the questions that are used in the research.[138] I have learned that this is the best method to obviously illustrate what has been going on and, as has always been the case, he agreed. After putting the questions to him there was a lengthy pause until he replied,

"Spiritual is about life and death and spirituality, well that's just how you are in the world."

As the conversation progressed he explained that everyone wonders about the existence of a God or a higher power, everyone wonders about the point in the world, about their point in the world, and everyone wonders what happens when they or others die. This is what 'spiritual' is. It is to ask these most profound of questions. Believing that there is a higher power doesn't define spiritual or spirituality anymore than not believing that there is a higher power defines them but what connects these things is not the answer. It is the question.

"There's lots of people who believe in God but that doesn't make them spiritual. Maybe we are all spiritual in a way because we all think about God, if God exists or whatever. Maybe there's something in us that makes us think about things like that..." [139]

The spiritual then is concerned with life and death, focussing on what might be considered philosophical questions. Spirituality is what follows from these questions.

"...spirituality is just the way we are spiritual..." [140]

Considering or deciding that there isn't a God or higher being affects who people are and what they do, as does considering or deciding that there is a God or higher being. One consideration is not better, more important or more spiritual than the other but both clearly evidence asking the question. Reaching or attempting to reach an answer to the questions play a significant role in who we are, what we think and how we act. This in no way diminishes the influence of birth or society in how we develop but considerations about God, an 'after life', or our life's purpose will influence much of how we see ourselves and of our decision making. Our thoughts, feelings and actions are our spirituality and evidence our answers or attempts to answer the 'spiritual questions'.

This could be open to the accusation of being cognitive, entirely focussed on the mind but that is to miss the point. People do not believe in life after death for necessarily cognitive, logical reasons. People do not believe there is a God or higher power for necessarily, cognitive, logical reasons. Sometimes, one way or another, people just *know*.

Of course this could be challenged with a scientific framework, but young people do not live their life with a scientific, entirely cognitive mindset. Young people are content to connect their mind and their emotions and make decisions and knowledge

75

claims on that basis. If anything, young people have a much more holistic knowledge frame. They are willing to include all their experience, all their cognitive considerations and all their emotions and feelings in decision making and knowledge claims.

Let me make it absolutely clear that even though the evidence is strong that young people give consideration to spiritual questions, this in no way suggests that they have faith, that they are interested in philosophy, Christianity or any other religion, or that they have awareness of any particular experience of any of these things. Young people ask the questions, and will continue to throughout the course of their lives. This does not mean that there is any sense of openness to religion, and to Christianity in particular.

The data is clear: Young people consider a group of questions. It is my contention that this is the sign of the spiritual in humanity and, considered alongside the evidence of 'spiritual experiences' in the general population, that this is a common human biological function. But, as Steve Bruce makes clear, biological 'needs' do not necessarily produce a single cultural solution.[141] Indeed, biological needs do not necessarily produce any solution. In my view, there is a universal biological 'spiritual' desire but this does not mean religion or faith of any kind will necessarily survive.

Young people's understandings are as wide and varied as the number of young people and we must therefore start from where they are. The understanding of the word God is different, of angel is different, of heaven, hell, creation, purpose, control, everything is as varied as the number of young people. The key then is to consider each young people uniquely and engage only with his or her meaning, his or her understandings.

Another key point here is that the 'answers' young people give to the questions are regularly associated with uncertainty. It is rare to find absolute certainty and this to means any engagement with the questioning of young people must be open and inclusive. It is likely that over time considerations and responses will change and not remain static. A simple example is in response to a death of say, a close family member. Even a religious person of strong faith will probably consider again if there is a God, where their relation is in death, and what this means to them. While this may encourage them in their faith, it is also quite possible that the faith will waver. The opposite is also true. In a similar situation, a person of no faith may begin to consider again if there is a God.

The responses to the spiritual questions will change and be affected by experiences in life. While this may create a variety of responses, the common thing is that young people consider the spiritual questions and the evidence of spiritual is the consistent desire to reflect on these things. This reflection is a significant part of the worldview of each young person and the spirituality of young people is how life is understood and experienced following this worldview.

[36] Kathryn, England
[37] Ian, Wales
[38] Mark, Wales
[39] Esther, England
[40] Alison, Northern Ireland
[41] Ross, Wales
[42] Darren, Scotland
[43] Becky, England
[44] Sam, England
[45] Lisa, Wales
[46] Hay, D. with Nye, R. (1998) *The Spirit of the Child* Zondervan, Page 6

[47] Simon, Scotland
[48] Though to what and for what reason is largely uncertain. This issue will be given greater consideration later.
[49] Danielle, England
[50] Robert, Wales
[51] Ian, Scotland
[52] Denise, Northern Ireland
[53] David, Scotland
[54] Chris, England
[55] I consider young peoples' reactions to religion in greater detail in a later section of this chapter.
[56] Catherine, Scotland
[57] Becky, England
[58] Naomi, England
[59] Chris, Northern Ireland
[60] Gillian, England
[61] Tori, Wales
[62] Sam, England
[63] Danielle, England
[64] Dawn, Northern Ireland
[65] Leanne, Scotland
[66] Ian, Scotland
[67] Nicola, Northern Ireland
[68] Matthew, Wales
[69] David, Wales
[70] Helen, England
[71] Kenny, Scotland
[72] Ryan, Northern Ireland
[73] Nathan, England
[74] Graham, Wales
[75] Lorraine, England
[76] Jamie, Northern Ireland
[77] Amanda, Scotland
[78] Robert, Wales
[79] Sheila, Wales
[80] Chris, Northern Ireland
[81] Amy, Northern Ireland
[82] Eleanor, Northern Ireland
[83] Mark, Scotland
[84] Jim, England
[85] Matthew, England
[86] Sheila, Wales
[87] David, Northern Ireland
[88] Debbie, Scotland
[89] Sarah, Wales
[90] Vicky, England
[91] Helen, Northern Ireland
[92] Ben, Scotland
[93] Adam, Northern Ireland
[94] Kate, Northern Ireland
[95] William, England

[96] Kyle, Scotland
[97] Linda, England
[98] Mark, Wales
[99] Matthew, Wales
[100] Kyle, Scotland
[101] Mark, Wales
[102] Alison, Northern Ireland
[103] John and Scott, Scotland
[104] Trevor, Scotland
[105] Nicola, Wales
[106] Alan, Wales
[107] Jamie, England
[108] David, Northern Ireland
[109] Steve, England
[110] Tanya, England
[111] David, Northern Ireland
[112] Sam, England
[113] Helen, Northern Ireland
[114] Laura, Wales
[115] Heelas, P. & Woodhead, L. (2005) *The Spiritual Revolution* Blackwell Publishing, Page 17
[116] Simon, Scotland
[117] Louise, Scotland
[118] Paul, Wales
[119] Chris, England
[120] Hay, D. with Nye, R. (1998) *The Spirit of the Child* Zondervan, Page 42
[121] Suzi, Scotland
[122] Gillian, England
[123] Catherine, Scotland
[124] Helen, Northern Ireland
[125] Chris, England
[126] Steve, England
[127] It is interesting to note that the Salvation Army are mentioned on a few occasions for their social work and the positive role that it has played in some young peoples' lives. There is however a clear distinction made between their 'positive' social work and their 'negative' church.
[128] Mike, England
[129] Adam, Northern Ireland
[130] Louise, Scotland
[131] Andrew, Wales
[132] Louise, Scotland
[133] Andrew, Wales
[134] Sandra, Scotland
[135] Patrick, Northern Ireland
[136] Catherine, Scotland
[137] Grace, Wales
[138] This took place following the conclusion of fieldwork so this particular conversation is not part of the research data.
[139] Darren, Scotland
[140] Claire, Wales
[141] Bruce, S. (2002) *God is Dead, Secularization in the West* Blackwell Publishing

The Future?

From this research it is very obvious that young people are asking spiritual questions and that they have a desire to reflect on their spirituality. There is also clear evidence that many young people are having extraordinary experiences that they do not fully understand but they have a desire to reflect on their spirituality. The difficulty lies not in the expressing, asking or reflecting but that space is not being provided so that young people can better undertake these activities.

Young people are spiritual in that they ask and desire to answer the spiritual questions and therefore they have spirituality. But this awareness of spirituality is often buried within the demands of every day life. Young people want to consider spiritual questions. They want to consider them so that they might better know what they believe and can connect this belief to life. But the space and opportunity to reflect is not being adequately provided. Some agencies are making efforts to provide the necessary space, both physical and emotional, but from this research I would have to say that they are not being very successful in their provision.

Young people have a lot to say and all that it took to open this up was to ask them at a good time and in the correct way. Within psychotherapy and psychoanalysis much time is given to the things that are buried within, especially in dealing with grief. It is argued that keeping things such as grief buried takes away energies that might be better used in life. Indeed many of these 'buried' emotions can manifest themselves in physical ways.

This raises a very straightforward question: If something is being buried among young people what affect, if any, will this have on the rest of life? Although at this point I'm unable to argue this with absolute certainty, I suggest that a lack of opportunity to reflect on important issues is leaving many young people unaware of their purpose and place in the world and that this is one of the root causes of some of the social difficulties found right across the U.K. Creating the opportunity to reflect as young people request is not going to suddenly solve all the current issues in society, but in my view it will certainly help.

It is essential for the development of young people that the correct space is provided to enable them to fully consider the spiritual questions and to connect to that which is currently 'buried'. Not to be told what the answers are, but a space where people can search and journey together to answer their questions. Indeed, a space where we all - old and young - can interact, learn one from the other and journey together as we explore for the answers to the spiritual questions and gain greater awareness of our spirituality. So, can these spaces be created?

Education

The main area relevant to education from this research is religious education. Because of the association that young people see between religion and spirituality, they often referred to religious education in their conversations about spirituality Practically every participant used Christian institutions and Christianity as their first point of reference and what is particularly concerning is the role of Religious Education in this process.

Young people are taking information that may be factually correct but are then making the assumption that this is the entirety of information about Christianity. Although there is only a little direct evidence of this in relation to other faiths, I would expect that other faiths are receiving the same treatment[142] and rather than aiding in the development of understanding and engagement with religion, Religious

Education is doing exactly the opposite. Young people are rejecting religious faith and spirituality on the basis of limited information and this needs to be addressed.

Rather than altering the content of the information provided in Religious Education or providing more information, the place of Religious Education should be completely reviewed. For those hoping to interest young people in religion, the truth is that Religious Education is a barrier rather than an encourager. All aspects of education except religious education are focussed on making young people into something - making them mathematicians, or scientists, or historians. Religious Education is most definitely not trying to make young people religious. And nor should it because in a school setting this would be wholly inappropriate.

The role of the education system needs to be clarified in this regard because the current system of education in the U.K. is largely result focussed. While I understand this and accept that is an entirely necessary role for education, this obviously does not allow much space, opportunity or time to grapple with spiritual questions or spirituality. Too much is being asked of Religious Education providers because while factually correct information is presented, there is inadequate space to reflect on this and this is creating negative reactions among young people.

To create this space would require a fundamental change in ethos and this would be asking too much. As long as the education system retains its emphasis on examinations and qualifications it will be difficult for the best spaces to be created and maintained so that spiritual questions and spirituality might be best considered. One possible way to overcome these difficulties is to alter Religious Education to achieve two things, or indeed into two totally separate areas of education:

1. Cultural Education: This title does not tell the whole truth but to date I have been unable to arrive at a more satisfactory title. The

U.K. is becoming more and more multi-cultural while conflict in various forms is rising between these cultures. I do not want to suggest that things are beyond repair. Indeed they are not even that bad, but the potential is certainly there for misunderstandings and prejudices to grow deeper resulting in greater conflict. Cultural Education would be one part of a response to this.

Rather than providing information focussed principally on religion, the subject would be much broader. Areas such as sports, arts, clothing, and history could be included to give a fuller picture of the different people in U.K. society, as well as those without.

Emphasis would need to be given to ensure that young people did not assume that the information provided was everything about any given culture or group in society. The primary focus in my view should be on interesting and exciting young people about the other people around them. This would include the people, old and young, from within their own cultural group as well as those without.

Religion would of course be a part of this subject, but young people would no longer be given the impression that this was all there was to know, nor would they be encouraged to make a choice about any given faith. This is a role for others outside the education system to fulfil. What Cultural Education would do is encourage openness among young people. It would emphasise the role of everyone in the development of culture and society while still providing the factual information that is currently part of Religious Education.

2. Spiritual Education: The system of education in the U.K. is largely authoritarian and has many power issues in the development of relationships. For that reason I do not think that it is the most suitable place for young people to consider spiritual questions and their own spirituality. Having said that, reflecting on spiritual questions is something that every person is doing and if this is going to play some part in education, then every person must be enabled to fully participate.

Once again I do not think that the term 'Spiritual Education' is adequate because connecting the words spiritual and education serves only to make this appear a step by step process where more knowledge is gained. I have also avoided using the phrase 'spiritual development' as this too suggests some being in some higher place than others. Every single individual that I spoke with had something to offer to the discussion. Every single individual had some feeling, thought or experience they could share and it is my view that phrases like 'spiritual development' or 'spiritual education' will diminish the role of these feelings, thoughts and experiences.

Some may prefer to consider this area as philosophy but I have shown in the previous chapter that these are fundamentally spiritual questions. They are questions that demand a response and young people consistently asked for opportunity to be provided where these questions could be considered. If it is the case that spirituality is about life, and is formed at least in part from spiritual questions, then the system of education should take this on board and find a way to encourage young people to fully consider and reflect. To use the phrase once again, education may have a key role to play in helping young people to connect lifestyle and belief.

My main concern about this whole area is the limitations that might be placed on it due to the education systems current emphasis on results. I accept that one of the key aspects of education is to teach people, to help them get qualifications and ultimately to be ready for employment. This is an important task but if it is the only role, then spiritual education has no place in school.

Philosophy and, to some extent, religion can be fully examined in a way in which spiritual education cannot. However, if spiritual education is about reflecting on questions of God, questions of existence and questions of death in order to connect these things to action in life, there is no place for examinations.

In a recent conversation with David Durston, a member of the Advisory Group for the Fellowship in the Spirituality of Young People, he suggested that Religious Education might be like teaching people the rules of football, the tactics of the game etc., examining them, but then not allowing them the time and space to play the game. The conversations in this Fellowship absolutely and certainly suggest that Religious Education is not a wholly positive influence in providing religious information or in enabling young people to consider spiritual questions and their own spirituality. This is very clear. What is not so clear is what Religious Education should be doing.

For too long representatives of religious institutions and many in education have accepted the value of Religious Education and I hope that this research might go some way to challenging that certainty. What I have sketched above is just that, a sketch. It is not complete in every detail and I put this recommendation forward more to begin a debate than to provide a concrete answer. There can be no doubt that Religious Education needs to change but I am still left wondering if it can ever change to allow the space and time necessary to reflect on spiritual questions and spirituality or would it be better to leave this to others?

Youth Work

There has been much debate regarding the place of spirituality in youth work and the participants in this research have much to offer in this debate, although perhaps indirectly. It is the case that spirituality is a part of life, and therefore a part of young people, and as youth work has developed with an emphasis on empowerment, participation and listening it would seem ideally placed to create the spaces and opportunities that young people request.

If we accept for the moment that considering spiritual questions and spirituality is a necessary component in the life of young people then it would seem that the youth service should provide for this. However, and this applies equally to any field working with young people, if the youth service does not accept that young people are spiritual or have spirituality, how would they be in a position to provide this service? Although not without difficulty, the education curriculum recognises and tries to define spirituality. On the other hand, rather than trying to clarify these terms and illuminate the impact they have on work with young people, many youth agencies have chosen to remove this area from aims and objectives.

It seems to me that to be active in this area one must have some awareness of one's own spiritual understanding, experience and spirituality. This does not mean the acceptance of absolutes, of God or of anything else, but for a youth worker to connect with young people in this area that youth worker *must* have some awareness of their own place in it. There *must* be some awareness of their own reactions to spiritual questions and to their spirituality, and to allow young people to search for their own answers without undue influence.

Young people ask for the space and opportunity to reflect on spiritual questions and their spirituality. The different aspects of a very broad youth service should be part of this provision but before engaging in 'spiritual youth work' the whole youth service would need to take account of its aims and objectives and then of its training. What place can 'spiritual education' play in youth work and how can this be reflected in future training? How are youth workers in training encouraged to reflect on the spiritual questions and on their own spirituality? How can youth workers be encouraged to engage and journey with young people as they attempt to answer their spiritual questions and reflect on their spirituality?

Engaging in 'spiritual youth work' requires a change in ethos that could take many years to achieve, if it is achievable at all. This is definitely something that should occur if all the needs of young people are to be met but at least in the short term, I think that others may better placed to provide this service.

Religious Institutions

For those who know me this may well come as some surprise, but in my view it is religious institutions that are best placed to engage with the spirituality of young people. There is a very clear reconnection in understanding of terms like religion, spiritual and spirituality and the main reference point used by young people is Christianity. But young people also have very strong negative feelings towards the Church

However, as I explained previously, part of the anger among young people is because they have expectations that are not being met. Young people are asking for space to reflect on important issues, on spiritual questions, on their spirituality and this space is not being afforded to them. There is a great opportunity for all religious institutions to respond to this desire but this must also be done in the right way.

First of all, each individual in the Church needs to be committed to the task. This is not the responsibility of ministers or youth workers, but is something that every one can and should be involved in. I know that youth workers in church and church related posts do much good work but to be honest I think this has become a profession largely because others are not doing it. My own view, and this is borne out in the methodology and findings of this fellowship, is that youth work is something that everyone can do and also that there are too many young people for them to be engaged with only by employed staff. Too often I have seen cases where churches don't know what to do with the young people in and out of the church so they decide to employ a youth worker. Once this is done no one knows how to support this new member of staff and often the people who were so committed to engaging with young people take a back seat because they expect that the youth worker will do it all.

Of course this is not in itself a reason for there not to be youth workers because it can be overcome by setting up the correct

87

structures. However, what the methodology of this fellowship has shown is that young people are not difficult to engage with if you are willing to listen and be in their space. To do this requires vulnerability but how much stronger might each of us become if we made the effort to step out side our own social situations and engage with other people, both young and old?

Each individual in the Church needs to take up the challenge presented by both the findings of this fellowship and the methodology. A radical shift in attitude and in the focus of the whole Church is required if the spiritual questioning of young people is not to become even further buried beneath the weight of modern life. Each individual needs to have a voice and play a part in engaging with young people to find ways to create the safe space to ask questions and to seek answers.

This is a process that everyone should be involved in and that needs to be facilitated by people not interested in control. The whole Church, as a large institution and each individual member, must move from the 'jug and cup' teaching method to a much more bottom up approach. Every person must be prepared to listen, to be changed and to journey with others to seek new ways of being.

If I realised anything as I went around engaging young people it was that all that I needed to do was to be there and ask some searching questions. Some might think that we need to build trust before we can engage at high levels of personal disclosure but this methodology shows that this isn't the case. Suzi and I talked for only a few moments before she disclosed her suicide story. What a privilege it was to be part of that and to feel like she had been waiting for years to talk about it with someone who really wanted to listen. There are many more cases of this type of situation in the conversations and the question I have is this: How many other people, young and old, are out there just waiting to be heard?

One of the key aspects of any successful work I have been involved in, whether with young people or adults, has been the emphasis on reflection. As I listened during the conversations I could not help but reflect on young people's responses and what they meant to me. Within the conversations that form the basis of this research the importance of encouraging immediate reflection among the young people is absolutely key. This was invaluable in gaining insight into young people's thoughts and feelings about spirituality but there is something unknown and unquantifiable that is equally important.

There is no doubt that the young people with whom I engaged will discuss the conversations further. This may begin initially as a general discussion about some guy coming up and talking to the group, but the depth of the disclosure during the conversation is likely to create further discussion of some important issues. Religious people must find a way to continue to be part of this discussion so that others might be supported in answering spiritual questions considering their own spirituality and connecting their life and belief.

Indeed we need to be part of that discussion so that we might be better able to answer spiritual questions, consider *our* spirituality and connect our life and belief. We need to trust that other people, young and old, know some things and have experiences that we can hear and be affected by. As much as I might want to encourage young people to take their spiritual questions and spirituality seriously, I want to hear from them so that I too might know something more of things that I only know in part.

142 See also Bruce, S. (2002) *God is Dead, Secularization in the West* Blackwell Publishing

And Finally...

There is much to consider in the findings of the Fellowship and although I have targeted only three areas I want to make it clear that the onus is on everyone to respond to it. Young people are asking for space and opportunity to consider spiritual questions, among other things, and the methodology of this Fellowship has shown how it can be achieved. But this is something that every individual person, including me, should be doing.

Although I travelled around the U.K to spend time with young people, there are young people everywhere. They are in your local town and at the end of your street. They are in your local park or on the football pitch. But even more importantly, for many readers there will be young people even closer than that. If you are a parent, grandparent, aunt, uncle or even a brother or sister, you will know young people and you should be making every effort to create the time, space and opportunity for them.

Indeed, this goes beyond just young people. I contend that at some point in life, every person of every age and every walk of life has asked spiritual questions and therefore has spirituality. For that reason, we should be creating the time, space and opportunity for people of all ages and all walks of life. The fundamental question is, having heard what young people have to say and seen the impact of the methodology of the Fellowship in the Spirituality of Young People, how are you going to respond?

The Young People

Over 200 young people participated in this research and below you will find details of approximately 50 of these young people. These young people are those who have been quoted in this text and while a large number of young people are being left out of this section, this in no way diminishes the role that they have played. Suzi's story may have featured prominently but her role is no more or less important than any of the other young people who allowed me to converse with them.

The details below will enable you to see some of the diversity of participants and perhaps to understand something more of the voices of all the participants.

Wales

1. Alan: Aged 18. Met in a bar in North Wales. Into skateboarding. Currently at University

2. Andrew: Aged 14 from a large farming family. Was still at school and was looking forward to leaving his home at the first available opportunity.

3. Claire: Aged 21 and currently unemployed. Had recently returned to Wales from six months on an employment scheme in Canada. She lived in a small village in central Wales and I met her in a café with friends.

4. David: I met David and his friends playing football in a park in North Wales. It was a hot day and during a break from the game the group agreed to talk to me. He was 15 and his favourite team was Liverpool. He had dreams of playing for them someday....although any team would do!

5. Graham: Was part of a group of four guys that I met in Cardiff on a night out. They were from a small town some way from Cardiff and

all considered themselves to be rural. Aged 22, he was a mechanic in his home town.

6. Grace: Aged 18, we met on the sea front in North Wales. Grace and her three friends were spending the day in the sun! She worked in a local hotel and restaurant when not at college completing a beauty course.

7. Laura: From North Wales and also worked in local hotel. This however was her full time employment. Aged 21, Laura was originally from a small village about 40 miles from the North Wales coast and Welsh was her first language.

8. Lisa: Aged 24, I met her on a walk with two male companions. She grew up in a city in South Wales but now lived and worked in the country in outdoor pursuits.

9. Mark: I met Mark in a bar in Cardiff. He was at University studying International Development and had recently spent time in the USA. He was aged 25

10. Matthew: I met him along with Alan and Sheila in North Wales. He was aged 19 and, like Alan, was a skateboarder.

11. Nicola: Was aged 22. Although still at college, she hoped to marry a rich man and raise children.

12. Paul: Aged 18, Paul was a courier in South Wales.

13. Ross: Aged 15 from Llandudno in North Wales. I met Ross and his sister in the airport on their way to Northern Ireland.

14. Sarah: A youth worker in a rural community in Central Wales. She was aged 22 and I met her in a café.

15. Sheila: Was 19 and, unlike her two male friends, was no longer into skateboarding! She did still hang around in that social group and although she had been a regular church attendee when she was young, she no longer attended.

16. Tori: From a small town in South Wales and was a Goth. She was aged 17 and I met her and some friends standing outside a shop.

Scotland

1. Amanda: Aged 15, she is a Goth from Inverness. She was in education and I met her with some friends hanging around a bus station.

2. Ben: He was working in the music industry and was trying to open his own studio. Aged 22 I met him in a bar.

3. Catherine: I met her and two friends in a small village on the east coast. She was aged 21 and training as a primary teacher.

4. Darren: Aged 19, I met him in a park with Ian and Simon. They were playing football on their day off from work. Darren owned a computer business and Ian worked for him.

5. David: Aged 24 he just moved to a new teaching post in a small village in the very north of Scotland. He was originally from near Carlisle.

6. Debbie: Aged 22, she had previously been a Christian but no longer perceived herself in this way.

7. John: I met John and Scott sitting on a wall on the outskirts of a housing estate in Edinburgh. Both guys were poorly paid and worked as security guards at a local factory. He is 19.

8. Kyle: I met Kyle in a bar where he was a bar man. He was aged 22 and was studying geography at university in Glasgow but was originally from the highlands from Scotland

9. Leanne: Aged 14, Leanne was still in education and hoped to remain there and go on to university to train a doctor.

10. Louise: I spoke to Louise and Sophie in a nightclub in Aberdeen. Now aged 22, she had grown up in the city but was studying law in Edinburgh.

11. Kenny: Aged 16, I met him being asked to leave a shopping mall with two friends, Daniel and Mary. He had recently left school and was not employed when I spoke to him.

12. Simon: I met him with Darren and Ian playing football. He worked for the local council, managing a gym in a leisure centre. He was aged 19.

13. Suzi; is 24 years old from an urban background in Scotland. She has an M.Sc and is currently studying for a Ph.D in a scientific discipline. She was part of a group of three female young adults, the other two participants being Lorna and Carrie. I met them in a restaurant in Edinburgh.

14. Trevor: I met him with Amanda in Inverness. He was aged 16 and also a Goth.

Northern Ireland

1. Alison: I met Alison with a friend, Helen on a train. She was aged 22, Catholic and recently returned from a tour to Australia.

2. Denise: Aged 21 from Belfast. She worked as a counsellor, especially with young people.

3. Chris: He was aged 18 and part of a group of four young men who described themselves as loyalists. They were part of a very strong social group.

4. Dawn: Aged 18, she was completing her A-levels at a school in Belfast. I met her and two friends, Nicola and Judith in a bar in Belfast.

5. Ryan: Describing himself as a republican, I met him Brendan, Sean and Melissa on a bus. Ryan was aged 22 and worked as a builder.

6. Jamie: Jamie lived in a small village outside Enniskillen. He was aged 17 and was at a technical college studying to be a plumber.

7. Amy: Aged 17, I met her outside the City Hall in Belfast, a regular hangout for Goths in the city. She was with Liam and Neil, two

friends who were also Goths. I met them after work. Amy was a secretary in a local bank.

8. Eleanor: Aged 21, Eleanor was employed as a teaching assistant and hoped to go on to train as a teacher. I spoke to her and Karen at a house party.

9. David: He came to my home to do some repairs when the conversation took place. He was aged 25 and, because of the death of his father, he had recently separated from his girlfriend.

10. Adam: Chris and Adam were friends and I met with a group of 4 young men on a street corner. He was aged 19 and worked in estate agency.

11. Kate: I spoke to Rose, Anne and Kate in a park in Coleraine. Aged 24, Kate was a Sunday School teacher in a small rural Church.

12. Patrick: I met Patrick and three of his friends in a bar in Newry. He was an accountant and lived in the town.

England

1. Chris: Gillian and Chris, both aged 19, were in Waterstones purchasing books on magic when I first spoke to them.

2. Esther: I met Danielle, Tanya and Esther in a bar in Newcastle. They were all 25 years of age and worked together in a solicitors in the city.

3. Helen: Aged 16, from Brighton, Helen worked in a café. I met with her and 3 friends in the café.

4. Jim: Jim lived in a small village on the coast on the south-west of England. Aged 22, he and a friend had recently purchased a small hotel that they hoped to renovate and manage.

5. Kathryn: She worked in the British Museum and had just finished work when I met her and some friends in a café on Tottenham Road, London. Aged 22, Kathryn lived in the city centre but had grown up in Leeds.

6. Lorraine: She and I conversed in the centre of Hull, although she was from a small town outside the city. Aged 14, she was still at school, and she was with her boyfriend when we met.

7. Matthew: He was completing his A - Levels when we spoke. I met Kirsty, Jim, Edward and Matthew in a coffee shop in Salisbury after school. Matthew was 18 years of age.

8. Nathan: Aged 14, Nathan was still in education but expected to leave school as soon as possible so that he could work in the family business. He was with Linda, also age 14, when I met him.

9. Sam: Becky and Sam, aged 24, were on a train to Cardiff when we spoke. To use her words, she was 'doing a crappy job' because she intends to go travelling next year

10. Steve: A fan of Hip-Hop, we met in Nottingham during his lunch break. Aged 24, he manages a small record label and is also a recording artist.

11. Vicky: Leslie, Gerry and Vicky were together when I spoke to them in Starbucks in Bristol. She was age 18 and at Bristol University studying psychology.

12. William: A 16-year-old skate boarder, from Liverpool whose second love was Everton Football Club. He had left school to work in his father's decorating business

References

Allan, J (1995) 'Popular Religion', in Francis, L.J., Kay, W., Kerbey, A. and Fogwill, O. (Eds.), *Fast-Moving Currents in Youth Culture* Oxford

Banks, Sarah (ed.) (1999) *Ethical Issues In Youth Work* Routledge

Becker, Howard S. (1998) *Tricks of the Trade* The University of Chicago Press

Bellah, Robert N., Madsen, Richard, Sullivan, William M., Swidler, Tipton, Steven M. (1985) *Habits of the Heart* University of California Press

Berg, Bruce L. (1989) *Qualitative Research Methods For The Social Sciences* Allyn & Bacon

Best, R. (Ed.) (1996) *Education, Spirituality and the Whole Child* Cassell

Bridger, Francis (2001) *A Charmed Life - The Spirituality of Potter World* Darton, Longman & Todd

Brierley, Peter (1999) *U.K. Christian Handbook: Religious Trends* Harper Collins

Brierley, Peter (2000) *The Tide is Running Out* Christian Research

Brown, Callum (2001) *The Death of Christian Britain* Routledge

Bruce, Steve (1995) *Religion in Modern Britain* Oxford University Press

Bruce, Steve (2002) *God is Dead Secularization in the West* Blackwell

Bullough, D. P. (1987) *Teenage Belief Systems* Open University, PhD

Chopra, Deepak (2000) *How To Know God* Harmony Books

Collins, Sylvia *Spirituality and Youth* in Martyn Percy (2000) Calling Time Sheffield Academic Press

Cox, E. & Cairns, J. (1989) *Reforming Religious Education: The Religious Clauses of the 1988 Education Reform Act* Kogan Page

Coupland, Douglas (1991) *Generation X* Abacus

Cuppit, Don (1997) *After God* Weidenfeld & Nicolson

Davie, Grace (1994) *Religion in Britain Since 1945: Believing Without Belonging* Blackwell Publishing

Deloria, Jr., Vine (1992) *God is Red A Native View of Religion* Fulcrum Publishing

Delgatto, Laurie (Ed.) (2003) *She Said...He Said...* Saint Mary's Press

Denscombe, Martyn (1998) *The Good Research Guide* Open University Press

Drury, Nevill (1998) *The Visionary Human* Element Inc.

Erricker, Jane, Ota, Cathy, and Erricker, Clive (eds.) (2001) *Spiritual Education, Cultural, Religious and Social Difference* Sussex Academic Press

Farnell, R., Furbey, R., Shams, al Haqq, Hills, S., Macey, M., Smith, G. (2003) *'Faith' In Urban Regeneration? Engaging Faith Communities in Urban Regeneration* Joseph Rowntree Foundation

Flory, R., & Miller, D (Eds.) (2000) *Gen X Religion* Routledge

Fontana, David (2003) *Psychology, Religion, and Spirituality* Blackwell

Fowler, James W. (1981) *Stages of Faith* Harper

Fowler, James W. (1996) *Faithful Change* Abingdon Press

Francis, Leslie J., and Kay, William K. (1995) *Teenage Religion and Values* Gracewing

Francis, Leslie J., and Kay, William K. (1996) *Drift from the Churches: Attitude Toward Christianity During Childhood and Adolescence* (Religion, Culture and Society) University of Wales Press

Francis, Leslie J., Kay, William K. and Campbell, William (Eds.) (1996) *Research in Religious Education* Smyth & Helwys

Francis, Leslie J. (2001) *The Values Debate: A Voice from the Pupils* Woburn Press

Gibran, K. (1980) *The Prophet* Pan Books (Originally published in 1926)

Giddens, A. (1991) *Modernity and Self Identity* Polity Press

Giddens, A. (2001) *Sociology* Polity Press

Gilbert, Nigel (ed.) (1993) *Researching Social Life* Sage Publications Ltd.

Goodbourn, D. R. (1989) *Development of Religious Consciousness* Manchester, PhD

Green, David & Green, Maxine (2000) *Taking A Part young people's participation in the Church* The National Society/Church House Publishing

Green, Maxine & Christian, Chandu (1998) *Accompanying Young People on the Spiritual Quest* The National Society and Church House Publishing

Griffith-Dickson, Gwen (2000) *Human and Divine An Introduction to the Philosophy of Religious Experience* Duckworth

Griffiths, Leslie (2002) *Voices from the Desert* Canterbury Press

Grimbol, William R. (2000) *The Complete Idiot's Guide To Spirituality for Teens* Alpha Books

Hammond, Catherine (ed.) (1991) *Creation Spirituality and the Dreamtime* Millennium Books

Hay, David (1982) *Exploring Inner Space Is God still possible in the twentieth century?* Penguin Books Ltd.

Hay, David, with Nye, Rebecca (1998) *The Spirit of the Child* Harper Collins

Hay, David, and Hunt, Kate (2000) *Understanding the Spirituality of People Who Don't Go To Church* University of Nottingham

Hay D. & Hunt K. (2000) *Is Britain's Soul Waking Up?* In 'The Tablet', 24 June 2000

Heelas, Paul & Woodhead, Linda (2005) *The Spiritual Revolution* Blackwell

Henderson, A. E. (1990) *Spirituality and Religious Education* Warwick, MPhil

Holloway, Richard (2001) *Doubts and Loves What is Left of Christianity* Canongate

Johnson, P. J. (2000) *Spirituality in the Primary School; A Study of Teacher Attitudes* Wales, Lampeter, PhD

Lee, John (1991) *Spiritual Development: A First Step for Youth Workers and Young People*

Lynch, Gordon (2002) *After Religion: 'Generation X' and the search for meaning* Darton, Longman and Todd

Lynch, Gordon (2003) *Losing My Religion?* Darton, Longman and Todd

Marler, P. and Hadaway, C. (2002) *'Being Religious' or 'Being Spiritual' in America: A Zero-Sum Proposition?* Journal for the Scientific Study of Religion 41 (2)

Maslow, A. (1962) *Toward A Psychology of Being* Von Nostrand

Maslow, Abraham (1970) *Motivation and Personality* Harper & Row

May, Tim (1997) *Social Research* Open University Press

Mayo, B. with Savage, S. & Collins, S. (2004) *Ambiguous Evangelism* SPCK

McDaniel, Katie (1999) *A Guide To Youth Ministry* National Society/Church House Publishing

McKeone, Mary (1993) *Wasting Time in School* St Pauls

Moody, Harry R. & Carroll, David (1997) *The Five Stages of the Soul* Doubleday

Moss, Bernard (2005) *Religion and Spirituality* Russell House Publishing

Mukadam, M. H. (1998) *Spiritual and Moral Development of Muslim Pupils in State Schools* Birmingham, PhD

Nesbitt, Eleanor (1987) *Children's Experience of Religion: Issues arising from Study of 8-13 Year Olds* Alister Hardy Research Centre

O'Donohue, John (1998) *Eternal Echoes: Exploring Our Hunger To Belong* Bantam Books

Osborne, Richard and van Loon, Borin (1999) *Introducing Sociology* Totem Books

Passmore, Richard (2003) *Meet them where they're at* Scripture Union

Peck, M. Scott (1990) *The Different Drum* Arrow Books

Peck, M. Scott (1993) *Further Along The Road Less Travelled* Simon Schuster Inc.

Richter, Philip, and Francis, Leslie J. (1998) *Gone But Not Forgotten* Darton, Longman and Todd Ltd.

Reddie, Anthony G. (2003) *Nobodies to Somebodies: A Practical Theology for Education and Liberation* Epworth Press

Robinson, Edward (1977) *The Original Vision A Study of the Religious Experience of Childhood* The Religious Experience Research Centre, Oxford

Robinson, Edward, and Jackson, Michael (1987) *Religion and Values at Sixteen* Plus Alister Hardy Research Centre and Christian Education Movement

Rodger, A. R. (1990) *Religion, Education and Human Spirituality* Stirling M Litt

Roof, Wade Clark (1999) *Spiritual Marketplace: Baby Boomers and the Remaking of American Religion* Princeton University Press

Rogers, Carl R. (1995) *A Way of Being* Houghton Mifflin Company

Rogers, Carl (1945) *The Nondirective Method as a Technique for Social Research* American Journal of Sociology, 50

Schermer, Victor (2003) *Spirit & Psyche* JKP

Schneiders, Sandra M. (Nov. 2003) *Religion vs. Spirituality: A Contemporary Conundrum* Espiritus

Sheldrake SJ, Philip (1991) *Spirituality and History* SPCK

Sheldrake SJ, Philip (1998) *Spirituality and Theology* SPCK

Spencer, Nick (2003) *Beyond Belief?* LICC

Strinati, Dominic (1995) *An Introduction To Theories of Popular Culture* Routledge

Strommen, Merton P. (ed.) (1971) *Research on Religious Development* Hawthorn Books

Tacey, David (2004) *The Spirituality Revolution* Brunner-Routledge

Tamminen, Kalevi (1991) *Religious Development In Childhood and Youth, An Empirical Study* Academia Scientiarum Fennica, Helsinki

Thorne, Brian (1998) *Person-centred Counselling and Christian Spirituality* Whurr Publishers

Tompkins, Ptolemy (2001) *The Book of Answers* Bloomsbury

Various Eds. (1990) *New Methods in R.E. Teaching: An Experiential Approach* Oliver & Boyd

Ward, Pete (1996) *Growing Up Evangelical* SPCK

Watts, Fraser, Nye Rebecca, and Savage, Sara (2002) *Psychology for Christian Ministry* Routledge

Willows, S. A. (1997) *Promoting Spiritual Development Through Religious Education in the First School* Durham, MA

Wright, Andrew (2000) *Spirituality and Education* Routledge

Youth A Part; Young People and the Church National Society and Church House Publishing (1996)

Journal of Youth and Theology International Association for the Study of Youth Ministry (2002 - 2003)

The Spirituality of Young People The Way Supplement (Autumn 1997)